The Case for a
Four-Day Week

The Case For series

Sam Pizzigati, *The Case for a Maximum Wage*

Louise Haagh,
The Case for Universal Basic Income

James K. Boyce, *The Case for Carbon Dividends*

Frances Coppola,
The Case for People's Quantitative Easing

Joe Guinan & Martin O'Neill,
The Case for Community Wealth Building

Anna Coote & Andrew Percy,
The Case for Universal Basic Services

Gerald Friedman, *The Case for Medicare for All*

Pavlina R. Tcherneva,
The Case for a Job Guarantee

Anna Coote, Aidan Harper & Alfie Stirling,
The Case for a Four-Day Week

Anna Coote
Aidan Harper
Alfie Stirling

———————

The Case for a
Four-Day Week

polity

The right of Anna Coote, Aidan Harper and Alfie Stirling to be identified as Author of this Work has been asserted in accordance with the UK Copyright, Designs and Patents Act 1988.

First published in 2021 by Polity Press

Polity Press
65 Bridge Street
Cambridge CB2 1UR, UK

Polity Press
101 Station Landing
Suite 300
Medford, MA 02155, USA

ISBN-13: 978-1-5095-3964-2
ISBN-13: 978-1-5095-3965-9 (pb)

A catalogue record for this book is available from the British Library.

Library of Congress Cataloging-in-Publication Data
Names: Coote, Anna, author. | Harper, Aidan, author. | Stirling, Alfie, author.
Title: The case for a four-day week / Anna Coote, Aidan Harper, Alfie Stirling.
Other titles: Case for a 4 day week
Description: Cambridge, UK ; Medford, MA : Polity Press, 2021. | Series: The case for | Includes bibliographical references and index. | Summary: "How a longer weekend can make us happier, healthier and greener"-- Provided by publisher.
Identifiers: LCCN 2020026325 (print) | LCCN 2020026326 (ebook) | ISBN 9781509539642 (hardback) | ISBN 9781509539659 (paperback) | ISBN 9781509539666 (epub)
Subjects: LCSH: Workweek. | Quality of work life. | Work-life balance. | Time management.
Classification: LCC HD5106 .C666 2021 (print) | LCC HD5106 (ebook) | DDC 331.25/722--dc23
LC record available at https://lccn.loc.gov/2020026325
LC ebook record available at https://lccn.loc.gov/2020026326

Typeset in 11 on 15 Sabon by Servis Filmsetting Ltd, Stockport, Cheshire
Printed and bound in Great Britain by CPI Group (UK) Ltd, Croydon

For further information on Polity, visit our website: politybooks.com

Contents

Acknowledgements

Many thanks to Eda Yazıcı for her extremely helpful additional research.

We are also grateful to the Communication Workers' Union for supporting the New Economics Foundation's work on a four-day week.

1

Introduction

It is often said that 'time is money', but time is far more precious than that. Even if we don't have money, we always have time. It's a finite resource because we don't live forever – and in that sense it's all we've got, or all we can be sure of. How we experience our time and how much control we have over it are of the utmost importance to all of us.

Article 24 of the Universal Declaration of Human Rights (UDHR) states: 'Everyone has the right to rest and leisure, including reasonable limitation of working hours and periodic holidays with pay.' But what is 'reasonable' and how much 'rest and leisure' is enough? In this book we set out arguments for a four-day week because we think the world would be a better place – and our lives would be much improved – if we spent less time working for money and had more time at our own disposal.

Would that appeal to you? Here are just a few of the answers we might expect:

Yes, please! I'm totally worn out working five days a week.

Four days would be a lot better than no days at all.

No thanks. I need more work, not less, to make ends meet.

I'd love more time off work, but not if it means less pay. I want more money to live a better life.

The boss wouldn't stand for it. I'd end up trying to squeeze five days' work into four.

So it's not a simple proposition. And therefore the 'four-day week' in our title is shorthand for a more nuanced set of proposals. Our aim is to reduce the hours that anyone is obliged to work to earn a decent living – to four days or around 30 hours a week or the equivalent across a year. How people allocate their paid working time should be as flexible as possible to suit their own requirements. We don't envisage a compulsory four-day week for all, but the gradual introduction of a range of measures to reduce working time in ways that benefit everyone by improving the quality of their lives. Throughout the following pages, we use the terms 'a shorter working week' or 'reduced working time' interchangeably to convey this idea.

Introduction

It may mean a year's worth of three-day weekends, or five 'spare' afternoons every week, or even
a longer break if the extra hours can be banked and
redeemed for a week or more at a time. You can
spend this in any number of ways. You can look
after your kids, visit your mum, hang out with your
friends, study a course, run round the park, put
up shelves, paint pictures, invent a new app, join a
band or a campaign group, learn to dance, play the
bazooka – you name it.

Most people like the idea of spending less time in
paid work. UK surveys published in 2019 showed
that 70 per cent of employees believe a four-day
week would improve their mental wellbeing,[1] and
64 per cent of businesses supported the idea of
adopting a four-day week.[2] Understandably, there's
more enthusiasm among employees if they anticipate no cut in take-home pay.[3] But according to the
Trades Union Congress, more than 3 million people
in the UK would like to work fewer hours even if
it would result in less pay, and 10 million people
would like to work fewer hours overall.[4] It's not
that people are work-shy. On the contrary, having
access to decent work is closely linked to wellbeing
and happiness.[5] However, people want more time
to use as they wish. You won't find many who are
longing to spend more hours at work, unless it's to

earn extra money (and we'll come to that). Some have regrets about how they have led their life, but it's rare to find someone who says 'I wish I'd spent more time in the office'.

Yet there is a kind of collective addiction to long hours of hard graft, a belief that it's good for us all and the only way to keep the show on the road. In a letter to *The Times* in November 2019, a retired consultant radiologist deplored the UK Labour Party's pledge to introduce a four-day working week. The NHS had already been 'brought to its knees', she declared, by limiting the hours of junior doctors to 56 a week. A four-day week would seriously damage their education 'and possibly sink the health service'.[6] This may be an extreme case, but it illustrates the point that many of us have found it hard to imagine a satisfactory alternative to the status quo. Whether the working week lasts for 40 hours or much longer, what is 'normal' has usually been perceived as natural or inevitable and, by implication, right and irreversible. That's a long way from the truth – and if anyone doubts that, just think how far the 2020 COVID-19 crisis disrupted everyday normalities in countries across the world.

Introduction

Where did 'normal' come from?

So let's take a closer look at how our current ideas about 'normal' took shape. In nineteenth-century Britain, a regular working day ranged from 10 to 16 hours, typically for six days a week. From the mid-nineteenth century onwards, workers on both sides of the Atlantic campaigned for a 'just and sufficient' limit to their hours of labour. The eight-hour movement gathered strength, and workers came out in their thousands to demand 'eight hours for work, eight hours for rest, eight hours for what you will'.[7] Karl Marx maintained that shortening the working day was a 'basic prerequisite' of what he described as the 'true realm of freedom',[8] and this became a central issue for socialist and labour movements in industrialized countries across the world.

In 1856, stonemasons in Melbourne, Australia, fought successfully for an eight-hour working day – a global first.[9] In 1889, gas workers in East London became the first to do so in Britain. In 1919, the nascent International Labour Organization (ILO) set out its Hours of Work (Industry) Convention, establishing the principle of an eight-hour day, or 40-hour week, which has since been ratified by 52 countries.[10]

In 1926 the US Ford Motor Company was one

of the first major employers to adopt a five-day, 40-hour week for workers in their factories – with no reduction in pay. Productivity increased and the corporation went from strength to strength.[11] In 1930, the cereal magnate W. K. Kellogg replaced three daily eight-hour shifts at his plant in Battle Creek, Michigan, with four six-hour shifts. Results included big cuts in absenteeism, turnover and labour costs, and a 41 per cent reduction in workplace accidents.[12]

Franklin D. Roosevelt launched his 'President's Re-employment Agreement' in 1933, urging US employers to raise hourly wages and cut the length of the working week to 35 hours. Roosevelt shared the view of UK economist John Maynard Keynes that government spending could stimulate the economy and that there was a strong relationship between higher productivity and shorter hours of work. He hoped to get more people back into work and – by raising wages at the same time – boost consumption and growth. Firms readily signed up, and between 1.5 million and 2 million new jobs were created.

A combination of industrial struggles and government initiatives ensured that the two-day weekend and the 40-hour week were widely adopted as standard by the middle of the twentieth century. But it wasn't all plain sailing. Average working hours continued to fall, as Figure 1 indicates, but less steeply from the 1980s. After that, the trend flattened in many countries and in some went into reverse.

In 1930, Keynes famously predicted that a 15-hour week would be the norm by the twenty-first century – how wrong he was! What happened to put a brake on progress towards reduced working time? A combination of economic and cultural develop-ments have locked us into the eight-hour day norm.

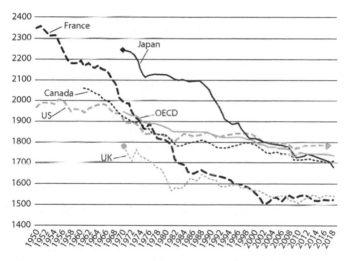

Figure 1: Average annual hours actually worked per worker, 1950–2018, all G7 countries with data pre-1971 and the OECD average.

Source: OECD https://stats.oecd.org/Index.aspx?DataSetCode=AVF_HRS

Introduction

Economic developments

When Keynes made his ill-fated prediction, he assumed that economy-wide labour productivity – that is, gross domestic product (GDP) per hour worked – would rise to a level that enabled society's needs to be met while everyone spent far fewer hours in paid employment. He anticipated an era of 'material abundance', bringing with it a challenge to ensure that it would 'yield up the fruits of a good life'.

For three decades following the Second World War, productivity did indeed rise quickly. At the same time, collective bargaining played a prominent role in the wider economy; so too did public sector coordination. Partly as a result of this, gains from productivity growth were more evenly distributed across society, in terms of both rising pay and falling average working hours.

But from the 1980s, the rules governing advanced economies began to change. Rates of growth in labour productivity started to fall as overall levels of investment by firms and governments receded. The composition of industry also started to shift, with a decline in manufacturing and a rise of the service sector. Information and communications-based technology became increasingly dominant, but appeared to have lower marginal gains for measurable GDP growth than the improvements in manufacturing and production seen in earlier decades.

The economic pie was increasing more slowly overall. More crucially still, a larger share of it started to shift towards property owners and share-holders at the expense of workers. The capacity of trade unions to bargain for better pay and con-ditions was undermined, most notably in the UK during the 1980s but in other countries and decades as well. Overall, pay increased at even slower rates compared with returns on wealth. The average level of unemployment rose significantly. Income inequal-ity rose to unprecedented post-war heights across Europe and North America, and then stubbornly remained high through various manifestations of both 'left' and 'right' governments across different countries. The rate of progress towards more leisure time slowed down conspicuously.

The 2008 financial crisis fired the starting gun for a third major post-war evolution in power and reward across advanced economies. In the UK, for example, the long-run rate of productivity growth has dropped by two-thirds since 2008. This has been both cause and effect of a marked increase in low-paid, insecure work and a period of weak pay increases without precedent in modern records. One in six workers in the UK (more than five million people) are experiencing low pay alongside some form of insecurity at work;[13] many are trapped in a revolving door between low pay and no pay at all. Meanwhile, in many other countries – notably in Southern Europe – unemployment remains very high. Alongside these disturbing trends, reductions in the average working week have stalled since 2008 for the longest period since before the Second World War.

Cultural developments

Behind all this, a powerful confluence of ideas has shaped prevailing attitudes about what is 'right' as well as 'normal'. In 1926 – the same year Ford Motor Company introduced the five-day 40-hour week – Judge Elbert H. Gary, board chairman of the United States Steel Corporation, told the *New York Times* that the five-day week was impractical, uncompetitive and illogical, not only for steel workers, but for any other business. 'The commandment says, "Six days shalt thou labor and do all thy work." The reason it didn't say seven days is that the seventh day is a day of rest and that's enough.'[14]

Judge Gary's aversion to shorter hours drew on something much deeper than fear of commercial risk. He subscribed to a widely held belief that work was the God-given purpose of humankind. Where labour was brutal and coercive – as it so often was – it was helpful to distinguish between body and mind, as Descartes had suggested.[15] For if humans were made 'in the image of God', then their God-like essence could be safely located in the mind (or soul), which may be separate and immortal, leaving the mortal body to be honed and disciplined into a machine for the mines, mills and factories of industrial capitalism.

The mechanical clock was a vital component of that discipline. As clockwork became more reliable and widely used, it set the scene for what Marx identified as the commodification of time and what British historian E. P. Thompson described as the birth of 'industrial time consciousness'.[16] Industry required its human machines to operate predictably and reliably, in ways that could be measured, bought and sold.

According to time theorist Barbara Adam, the variable time of 'seasons, ageing, growth and decay, joy and pain' gave way to the 'abstract time of the clock where one hour is the same irrespective of context and emotion'.[17] We have since grown used to thinking about time in discrete, globally consistent units that can be counted uniformly – seconds, minutes, hours, days, weeks and so on. We live accordingly, staking out our lives by clock and calendar.

Clock time has served and strengthened a powerful work ethic that embraces the idea of hard work as a route to profit and success. This has deep roots in economic and cultural developments over several centuries. It has served modern capitalism well, but with increasingly toxic effects. For if long hours of paid work are the route to virtue and success, it follows that the main purpose and value of human existence is productive capacity. By this logic, those who are not 'productive' have no worth. Like wheat from chaff, hard-working 'strivers' are separated from lazy 'skivers'.[18] The former are rewarded, the latter punished – by increasingly ungenerous systems of 'social protection'.

There are many politicians and business leaders who now seem keen to reverse the trend of reduced working time. They brag about sleep deprivation, while energy drinks, late-night gyms and self-help books propagate an 'always on' culture of relentless productivity. Tycoon Elon Musk of PayPal and SpaceX declares that 'nobody ever changed the world on 40 hours a week'.[19] Jack Ma, Chinese billionaire and CEO of the Alibaba Group, champions a '996' routine of 9 a.m. to 9 p.m., six days a week.[20] All these attitudes have contributed to a strong cultural bias in favour of long hours of work.

We can change what is 'normal'

However, on both fronts – economic and cultural – there are some encouraging signs. Across advanced economies today, higher productivity is in fact associated with *lower* annual hours worked. Poorer countries such as Greece and Mexico are at one end of the spectrum, with higher annual hours and comparatively low productivity, while North European and Scandinavian countries sit at the other end, with higher productivity and lower annual hours. Countries such as the UK sit among high-productivity economies, but even here there are significant differences *between* countries. Consider the gap that exists between Germany and the UK, for example: in 2018 average annual hours worked per capita in Germany (1,363) were much lower than in the UK (1,538) while GDP per hour worked was much higher (109 compared with 103).[21] No wonder people quip that German workers could lay down tools sometime around Thursday lunchtime and still get as much done as UK workers would by the end of Friday.

Comparing productivity across nations is problematic because it assumes a constant and comparable measure of price and value. But there is evidently no single set of rules for configuring an economy. There is no law for the number of working hours required to generate 'success'. What matters is not just productivity, but who gains and how. The relationship between time spent working and other economic fundamentals may have significant path dependency, underpinned by culture and institutions. But history shows us that countries can – and do – change course. That's because decisions and actions by politicians, trade unions and wider civil society really make a difference.

And we are not destined to be locked in forever by cultural bias. Unless we believe, with Judge Gary, that there's a God-given standard for hours of work (and we don't), we can agree that it is socially constructed – and therefore we can change it.

There is nothing 'normal' or 'inevitable' about doing paid work for five days or 40 hours a week. Nor should the process of selling our time control and shape all other aspects of our experience. We reject the assumption that we live to work, work to earn, and strive to earn more in order to buy more things because that's supposed to be good for the economy. After all, the whole point of economic activity is to serve the interests of people and the planet – not the other way around.

Too much work can ruin our health. Beyond a certain level, having more money doesn't make us any happier. Buying increasingly resource-intensive stuff risks breaching the limits of our finite planet and tipping the whole world towards catastrophe. Time is an asset to be nurtured and cherished. Unpaid time is far too valuable to be squeezed and shunted into small corners of our lives.

So these are strong reasons for moving towards a shorter working week, and they have been thrown into sharp relief by the social and economic effects of the 2020 COVID-19 pandemic.

In the next chapter we explore these reasons in more detail, in particular how reduced hours of paid work can bring benefits to society and the environment. In Chapter 3, we consider and respond to a range of challenges to our proposal, including questions about choice, leisure and pay, and whether reduced hours will be bad for the economy. In Chapter 4, we describe how it's done in practice – from government interventions and trade union negotiations to initiatives by individual employers and cross-sectoral campaigning. In Chapter 5, we set out a route map for the transition to a shorter working week.

2

Why We Need a Shorter Working Week

Sandra Andersson is employed at a Toyota service centre in Gothenburg, southern Sweden. She works the equivalent of a four-day week, putting in a six-hour shift for five days a week. Starting early at 6 a.m., she finishes at midday and has the afternoon to herself. She travels outside the rush hour, so her daily commute is quicker. And her pay is no less than it would be if she were working eight hours a day. 'It's wonderful to finish at 12', she says. 'Before I started a family, I could go to the beach after work – now I can spend the afternoon with my baby.'

Toyota was an early innovator. Until 2002, its service-centre workers came in at 7 a.m. and left at 4 p.m. They were often stressed and sometimes made mistakes. Customers complained of long waiting times. Then the work regime switched to provide two six-hour shifts, starting at 6 a.m. and at noon, without loss of pay. Workers were reportedly more contented, there was lower staff turnover and recruitment became easier. In 30 hours, mechanics produced 114 per cent of what they had produced in 40 hours, and profits rose by 25 per cent.[1]

Reducing work time can improve the quality of workers' lives and this in turn can improve the quality of their work. What happened at the Toyota centre is by no means unique. There are plenty of workplaces where hours have been cut without loss of pay, bringing positive results all round (see Chapter 4). In this chapter, we explore ways in which moving towards a shorter working week can help to address some of the most pressing challenges we face today – including poor health, unequal distributions of work and time, gender inequalities, transforming childcare and other public services, enriching democracy, and promoting ecological sustainability.

Health and wellbeing

Long hours and overwork are known to trigger severe levels of stress, which is one of the main reasons why people take sick leave. In the UK, for example, the total number of days lost in 2018 through absenteeism attributed to work-related stress, depression or anxiety was 15.4 million, an increase of nearly 3 million on the year before.[2] One in four of all days lost through illness was reported to be a direct result of workload. Days lost to work-related stress, depression and anxiety have been steadily increasing since 2014. Intense and over-long hours of work are a global phenomenon. In Japan, an estimated 10,000 workers are said to die every year as a result. Indeed, the problem even has its own name: *karōshi*.[3]

For every worker whose sick leave is officially recorded, there are many others who keep going in spite of the damaging effects of overwork. They suffer from fatigue and stress, which can increase the probability of errors and accidents as well as illness.[4] Overwork is costly for employers and erodes economic performance. More importantly, it damages the quality of people's lives and their ability to function well and flourish.

It follows that, for many of us, a shorter working week would improve our experience of employment, protect our health and enhance our wellbeing as well as the quality of our work. Several studies support this assumption (see, for example, pp. 69–71). The benefits for health and wellbeing are greater where hours are cut without loss of pay, but even when time is exchanged for a reduction in wages, or a smaller increase in pay, reduced working time is often found to reduce stress and other symptoms of poor mental health, with subsequent benefits for the quality of their performance at work.

Distributions of work and time

Much depends, of course, on what people are paid in the first place, whether their work is secure and how far they feel in control of their time. While some people are overemployed, others cannot get the hours they need to earn a decent living. In 2018, the number of people designated as underemployed in the UK stood at 2.39 million, while there were 10.24 million people who wanted to work less – although most did not think they could afford to do so: 6.66 million said they wanted fewer hours without loss of pay.[5] What's so obviously lacking is a fair distribution of working time, so that there's a chance for everyone to enjoy a balance between paid work and time off that suits their needs.

It is not only hours of work that are unequally distributed, but also pay and security. Since 2008, both the major growth in zero-hour contracts and the so-called 'gig economy' further complicate headline employment figures: where rising employment rates are interpreted as straightforward and positive economic or social outcomes, they can also conceal deep issues of low pay, precarity and *under*employment.[6]

Further developments in automation are likely to exacerbate existing inequalities in hours and income.[7] We don't anticipate the unemployment apocalypse that some predict: eye-catching calculations about the scale of lay-offs tend to conflate technical *feasibility* with the *probability* of what will actually happen. Nevertheless, it remains highly likely that automation will affect the distribution of paid work, increasing polarization in a two-tier labour market. Middle-income jobs that are highly structured, routine and repetitive, such as certain occupations in administration, legal professions and human relations, are among the most likely to be superseded by technology – because it is technically feasible to do so and marginal labour costs outweigh the capital costs of replacement. High-paying managerial roles and direct owners of some company shares are likely to benefit most from such changes. Meanwhile, low-paying, insecure work is likely to proliferate, as unprotected work through digital platforms multiplies, and as demand grows for domestic cleaners, personal trainers and other lifestyle services required by those whose incomes have been enhanced by new technologies.

Social and economic inequalities are bad for individuals' health and wellbeing as well as for society as a whole.[8] As Pickett and Wilkinson have demonstrated, outcomes for a range of health and social problems (physical and mental health, drug abuse, education, imprisonment, obesity, social mobility, trust and community life, violence, teen pregnancies and child wellbeing) are significantly worse in more unequal rich countries.[9]

Reduced working time can't solve all these problems. But it can play a vital role as part of a broader strategy to increase hourly rates of pay and improve employment conditions and job security in the gig economy. It can help to distribute paid work more evenly across the working population so that, instead of an ever-widening gap between the 'haves and have-nots', available work is spread in order that more people have access to a sufficient number of adequately paid hours of employment.

Reduced working time offers a useful strategy for avoiding lay-offs where jobs are threatened by automation. Increasingly, trade unions are negotiating shorter hours in response to such changes (see pp.80–6). The same applies when jobs are at risk in periods of economic downturn, when many organizations have cut hours across the workforce to avoid mass redundancies, at least until things pick up again. Even a temporary shift to shorter working hours can allow people to experience a different work–life balance and disturb the idea of what is 'normal'. It also keeps workers engaged with the labour market instead of their being laid off, if only for a limited period. Staying in paid employment means not having to depend on benefits or settle for insecure, low-paid work (if it can be found) where hours are either too short to make ends meet or too long to make a decent life possible. Even a relatively short spell of unemployment can lead to loss of skills and confidence as well as income, with associated risks to health and wellbeing.

We expect these effects to shift to a more permanent footing as the economy adjusts to long-term structural changes, such as the transition from fossil fuels to renewables. Where programmes such as the UK's Green New Deal are set in train, they are likely to recruit or redeploy large numbers of workers. Having a four-day week (or equivalent across a month, year or lifetime) as the default model for employment will expand job opportunities and limit inequalities. If these jobs are relatively secure and widely distributed, they can help to keep the economy on an even keel and reduce fluctuations in the labour market. As more people stay in paid work – with the important proviso that they earn an adequate income – it follows that fewer will have to claim social security benefits or be exposed to health risks associated with unemployment. Public funds that would otherwise need to be spent on income support and healthcare could instead be invested in (for example) improving other public services, and building a greener economy.

Paid and unpaid labour

Just as paid time is unequally distributed, so too is unpaid time – the everyday activities of caring, child-rearing, cooking, washing, cleaning and much else besides. This is the 'core economy', which provides an essential foundation for the formal economy.[10]

The core economy involves the reproduction of human assets and relationships. It is largely uncommodified and unpaid, routinely ignored and often exploited. Yet it has enormous value – indeed, without it, the formal economy could not function at all. A healthy society depends on nothing so much as the quality of relationships within it. Building and nurturing social relationships are central functions of the core economy and they take time: staying in touch, doing things together, helping each other, and simply enjoying the company of friends, neighbours and family. If all of us had more time for these relationships, there would be gains all round. Children could spend more time with their parents. Older and disabled people who can't manage on their own could become less isolated and more integrated with friends, neighbours and family – as would many who currently work too much. (It also matters that we look after ourselves, and that takes time too.)

The core economy can flourish and expand, or weaken and decline, depending on the circumstances and conditions within which it operates. When the formal economy devours too much human time in the workplace, it weakens and diminishes the core economy on which it depends.[11] Moving to a shorter paid working week could help it to flourish, by giving people more time to contribute to a range of vital activities that are not usually monetized or traded.

Gender relations

However, there is nothing inherently good or right about the core economy. Just as it shapes and sustains social and economic life, so too it can reflect and reproduce inequalities. Most obviously, activities in the core economy mainly involve women working without wages. Women take on low-paid jobs – often part-time, casual and precarious ones that have few opportunities for advancement – because much of their time is taken up with unpaid caring responsibilities. This generates a pattern of lasting inequalities between women and men in job opportunities, money and power.

In modern industrial and post-industrial economies, unpaid labour remains both highly gendered and persistently undervalued. It seldom features directly in traditional measures of economic 'progress', such as GDP or employment rates. Unpaid childcare and domestic labour are said to be worth the equivalent of 20 per cent of GDP, but there is no formal way of valuing these activities.[12]

Globally, women are responsible for 75 per cent of unpaid care and domestic labour.[13] Across OECD countries (Organisation for Economic Co-operation and Development), women do on average nearly twice as much unpaid work as men (4.24 hours a day for women aged 15–64, compared with 2.3 hours for men).[14] Although men typically do longer hours of paid work, when paid and unpaid working time are combined, women still work longer hours in most countries (exceptions are Denmark, the Netherlands, New Zealand and Norway).[15] They are also more likely than men to suffer the ill-effects of over-long hours of work, not only because of the combined pressures of paid and unpaid work, but also because they have relatively little power and autonomy in the workplace.[16]

The persistence of gendered inequalities – in spite of decades of campaigning and a considerable amount of legislation for equal opportunities – can be linked to the current structure of working time. From the 1960s onwards, as more and more women joined the paid labour force, they have been expected to do so in ways that interfere as little as possible with their traditional caring responsibilities. Many are consigned to low-paid, low-status, insecure employment because they opt for shorter hours or part-time jobs, or give up work for years at a time to look after children or elderly relatives. In 2019, the number of women in the UK working part time constituted 41 per cent of all women in employment, compared with 13 per cent of men.[17] Those who work part time are typically less well paid hour-for-hour than full-time workers at every level of qualification.[18]

Some women are financially supported by a male partner in paid employment, but this can be a mixed blessing. One study shows that 25 per cent of deprivation is caused by unequal distribution of resources *within* households, disproportionately affecting women.[19] And there is more than money at stake: there is also power, identity, capabilities and relationships. Being trapped in the margins of the job market robs women of opportunities to branch out, earn more and develop their full potential. And men lose out in some ways too. Being the 'breadwinner' cuts them off from important swathes of family experience and limits their chances to acquire skills and confidence in parenting and care. Inequalities between parents can breed resentment and conflict at home. Women and men rarely choose to live this way but are driven to it by force of custom and expectation.[20]

If part time became the new full time, all this could change. Our proposals for reduced working time are emphatically not about women doing fewer hours of paid work to achieve a better work–life balance. We want this for men too, as an essential step towards changing today's gendered pattern of time use.[21] An extra day a week would open up opportunities for men to learn how to care.

Of course, men who find themselves with extra free time will not automatically spend it on childcare or housework. Our aim is to shift expectations and create more favourable conditions for moving towards a new 'normal', where men and women share, where gender identities are not tied up with allocations of paid and unpaid labour, where men are no longer exiled for most of the week from their families and where women have a wider range of options for how to spend their time. Giving people – especially men – more time away from work is not sufficient to achieve this, but is nonetheless a necessary precondition.

Transforming childcare

A shorter working week for men as well as women could help to transform the economics of childcare, as well as gender relations. Childcare workers are predominantly female. The quality of childcare matters a great deal, whether it is carried out at home or in a social setting. It shapes the potential of future generations. As such, it is extremely valuable to individual children and families, and to society at large. Yet because childcare is often regarded as 'women's work' and closely associated with unpaid labour, it is far lower paid than many comparable jobs that are seen as 'men's work', such as those in construction and refuse collection.

The New Economics Foundation (NEF) and others have argued that childcare workers should have pay, training and career development on a par with primary school teachers, to reflect the social value of the work they do.[22] This is bound to raise costs, particularly if they also work a shorter working week. The impact on families' finances could be offset in two main ways: through more public investment in childcare as an essential service, affordable to all who need it; and by freeing up parental time through shorter hours of paid work.

To develop the second strand of this argument, NEF calculated the potential effects of both parents in a two-parent family working a four-day, 30-hour week, with each one spending the fifth day looking after their children. In this scenario, they would need formal childcare for three days, as opposed to the five days they would need if both parents worked a full-time five-day week. In theory, the arrangement could also free up capacity in childcare services so that more children have access. At the same time, it would start to make childcare a normal part of the weekly routine for fathers as well as mothers.[23] The point of this thought experiment (which is all it claims to be) is not that it is bound to happen, but that it's worth exploring ways in which shorter working hours could reshape the relationship between formal and informal care, between parents and children, and between women and men.

Co-producing public services

A shorter working week can release more time for informal caring, but our aim is certainly not to replace collectively provided services with uncommodified care. We want to create a new accord between paid and unpaid labour, where the two economies are mutually reinforcing, rather than one crushing or distorting the other.

Our proposal for a redistribution of time is part of a broader effort to transform public services so that they are not simply provided for people by service workers, but are designed and delivered in partnership with those who are expected to benefit from them. People who use services (and indeed anyone who might use them in future) have insights and experience that can help to make those services more relevant and effective in meeting individual needs. Engaging them in decision-making is crucial to improving the quality of services, and also enables them to take more control over what happens to them in the course of their own daily lives.

NEF has developed a radical redesign of public services known as 'co-production'. According to this, people who use (or may in future use) services, join forces with providers of services and form equal partnerships that combine lay and expert knowledge to develop ways of meeting needs. Co-production harnesses human assets beyond the paid workforce and so enriches the pool of resources available for delivering services. It does not diminish the role of service workers – although it calls for profound changes in the way they inter-act with others, shifting from a culture of 'caring for' to one of enabling and facilitating care for one another as peers.[24]

The critical point here is that co-production takes time. People whose daily lives are consumed by long hours of paid employment are unlikely to have many spare moments to enter into such partnerships or to engage in collective dialogue and decision-making. A shorter working week could make time for this and thereby help to build a more engaged and participative approach to a range of essential services – from education, health and care, to housing, transport and beyond – making them more responsive to people's needs and using public funds more effectively.

Taking control and enriching democracy

An important lesson from practical experiences of reduced working time (see Chapter 4) is that what matters most is not just having more disposable time, but having greater control over time. People really appreciate being able to determine what happens in their daily lives and not being entirely in thrall to forces they can't control – such as the demands of the economy. We all feel better when we have time to engage in autonomous activity, free from external control and influence, and in the company of those with whom we have close relationships.[25]

But because assets, opportunities and obligations are so unevenly shared between people, some have more freedom than others in how they dispose of their time. That is why moving to a shorter working week must be part of broader policy agenda that aims to give people greater control over their lives through a more equal distribution of resources – including money and power as well as time.

To build and realize a progressive agenda, we need a strong democracy at all levels of society. Shorter hours of paid work could release time to take part in community-based activities, to join local groups and to engage with local and national politics. Democracy takes time. For a start, if you want to make an impact on policymaking, you need time to get informed and think through the issues – by going to the local library or meeting up with others to talk it over, for instance – and to join in campaigns, sign petitions, lobby councillors and MPs, get active in a trade union, set up or join local voluntary activities and go on demonstrations. If long working hours make you too busy for this kind of thing, you are more likely to opt out and leave it to others. This can make the difference between a more inclusive, informed, deliberative politics and a manipulative, top-down populism that thrives on inertia and impulse. A passive, distracted or apathetic electorate is easy prey for the kind of oversimplified messaging and bandwagon rhetoric we have witnessed from the growing ranks of populist politicians across much of the world. Reduced working hours won't solve the problem on its own, but giving people more time to engage in dialogue and decision-making could help make democracy more textured, participative and rooted in everyday experience.

Safeguarding the environment

There is a strong correlation between long hours of paid work and high-carbon patterns of consumption,[26] and the relationship holds true even after controlling for the level of income.[27] Patterns of consumption are influenced not only by income, but also by how much time people have at their disposal. In general, the more hours we put in at work, the more we earn, and for many this is essential to make ends meet. For those on higher incomes, nonessential consumption rises disproportionately as a means of signalling social position. But equally, the more that any of us work, the more we also opt for resource-intensive 'convenience' products and services, rather than taking the time to do things for ourselves.[28] These dynamics can all cause unnecessary harm to the natural environment.

Time-poverty (or 'busy-ness') is another factor driving consumption.[29] The more hours we work each week, the busier we are, the more we seek out 'convenience' products to make life possible. We buy more packaged and processed ready meals, accumulate more labour-saving gadgets, travel by car or take a plane to save time, and summarily abandon and replace items that don't work. People at all levels of income can be uncomfortably short of disposable time, but higher earners can – and do – engage in a lot more of these 'fast-lane' activities, which are generally more carbon- and resource-intensive, more polluting, and more likely to include plastics and other non-recyclable materials, compared with alternatives based on a more sustainable rhythm of life where people have more time outside paid work.

High levels of consumption represent a desirable lifestyle deeply embedded in popular imagination. Not everyone lives that way, but many associate it with success and aspire to it. It's taken as a sign that you are doing your best and climbing the ladder, gearing up for promotion and a pay rise. Success is associated with earning more money and being able to buy more things. Buying more things is a sign of being successful – and so it goes on, ratcheting up consumption of resource-intensive products.

Having too little time at our disposal or relying largely on consumption for our path to happiness can drive us towards environmentally and socially damaging behaviours. It tends to be self-defeating: focusing on possessions, image, status and reward leads to unhappiness and discontent.[30] Yet it is what modern capitalism depends upon. Famously, US President George Bush responded to the 9/11 terror attacks in 2001 by urging Americans not to be afraid to carry on flying and shopping, and in 2006 he declared that his top goal was to keep the economy growing and, to that end, encouraged everyone 'to go shopping more'.[31]

There is, however, a growing consensus among climate scientists and environmental economists that 'business as usual', where the success of an economy is measured largely by growth in gross domestic product (GDP), cannot continue. What matters far more than a narrow measure of aggregate 'output' is the overall and distributed wellbeing of a population. One determinant of this is inequality in means (wealth and income). An increasingly urgent goal is to reduce greenhouse gas emissions and depletion of natural resources – especially in the rich world – to safeguard the natural environment, which itself is a fundamental determinant of human wellbeing. In democratic states this has to be achieved in ways that can win and maintain popular support, which calls for policies that do not impair the wellbeing of the population and do not exacerbate inequalities. Wherever possible, ecosocial policies should be developed that are mutually reinforcing, bringing benefits both to society and to the environment.[32]

Achieving the steep reductions in emissions that are required to meet internationally agreed targets will be contingent on significant shifts in industry, which in turn will have large knock-on effects for the labour market. This will lead to gains and losses in employment. For example, the kind of policies that are proposed in the UK's Green New Deal will (if implemented) create new jobs in such areas as renewable energy and retrofitting homes.[33] In other areas, such as fossil fuel extraction, there are likely to be job losses. Reducing the standard working week to four days, or introducing more flexible arrangements for people to work the equivalent in hours, could help to share out available paid employment among more people. This echoes the approach of trade unions trying to avoid lay-offs resulting from automation.

Juliet Schor is a leading expert on working time and its environmental effects. She rightly acknowledges that there is no simple equation between the number of hours reduced per week and the number of new employment opportunities. Schor and colleagues observe that 'the size of the employment effect will depend on how hours reductions affect the supply and demand of labor, via changes in wages and productivity', but there will nonetheless be some positive employment effects.[34] They point out that hours reduction can not only keep more people in employment, but is also a key factor associated with 'lower carbon emissions and other reduced environmental pressures'.[35] Several studies show a strong positive correlation between average working hours per week and carbon emissions. A review of 29 high-income countries published in 2012 found that those with fewer average work hours tend to have lower ecological footprints, carbon footprints and carbon dioxide emissions.[36] More recently, Schor and colleagues studied links between working hours and carbon emissions across 50 US states. They found that shorter hours of work were positively associated with lower state-level carbon emissions, and concluded that 'working time reduction allows a society to reduce its impact on the environment'.[37] Although this doesn't prove that one causes the other, the findings are nonetheless striking and warrant further research and investigation. The association is strong enough to suggest that moving towards a shorter working week is, at the very least, highly consistent with reducing harmful emissions and safeguarding natural resources.

Of course, there are other factors that can contribute to sustainability, notably changing technologies and more use of renewable energy. Indeed, over the past decade the relationship between hours and emissions has changed, with emissions falling while average working hours have increased. However, it is most unlikely – even if such trends continued – that production could be decarbonized far enough or fast enough to meet urgent climate mitigation targets. Patterns of consumption will almost certainly have to change, not just the supply of 'business-as-usual' goods and services.

Schor and colleagues distinguish between the 'scale effect' at macro-level and the 'composition effect', where shorter hours can encourage less carbon-intensive lifestyles through greater 'time affluence'.[38] The scale effect is where a long-term shift towards a shorter working week can help to reduce energy-intensive consumption by lowering the rate at which wages increase. Although trade unions are understandably committed to reducing hours without pro rata loss of pay, Schor envisages a gradual shift towards workers taking reduced hours in return for a smaller annual increment. The gradual and cumulative effect will be to slow the rate at which incomes increase, and consequently the amount that is consumed. 'The key issue here is controlling aggregate demand and, through it, the volume of production', she writes. 'Therefore we expect that countries which take a higher fraction of their productivity growth in the form of hours reductions will have lower ecological and carbon footprints, all other factors being equal.'[39] (Of course, Schor's 'scale effect', in terms of demand, is contingent on a continued relationship between production and emissions. The impact of aggregate demand could change if production processes became less carbon-intensive, for example through more use of renewable energy and an increasingly circular economy. But whether or how far that is likely to happen remains to be seen.)

The 'composition effect' is about changing patterns of consumption. If you have more time at your disposal, you are likely to do less 'convenience' shopping to cope with a busy schedule. You have time to walk and cycle, to take the train, to prepare and cook fresh food, to make and repair – rather than replace – things you need for daily living. When an entire workplace switches to a shorter working week, there are likely to be fewer daily commutes per person and less energy used in heating and lighting the workplace. This was one effect of the experiment in Utah, USA (see pp. 71–4), and has been supported through other studies.[40]

Once people start to experience more disposable time in exchange for labour, rather than just more money, the signals change about what constitutes success – influencing workers across the income spectrum, including those on lower pay who aspire to the rewards of the better off. There's no straightforward causation here, but there is a chance to shift the dial, to enable more of us to change perspective, pause and reflect, and value things differently. It's one thing to have enough of what you need to live a good life: everyone should be able to do that. Fetishizing long hours of work as a means of accumulating consumer goods and multiplying carbon-intensive activities is quite another. A world with more disposable time could help us all to get out of the fast lane, cut emissions, buy fewer resource-intensive consumer products and think again about what really matters in life. We could learn to value time not just money and favour sufficiency over excess.

3

Some Challenges

The case for a shorter working week is bound to raise some challenging questions. We are often asked about personal choice – what if people want to work longer hours? Some doubt whether giving people more disposable time will in fact reduce damage to the environment. Some object on the grounds that a shorter working week means earning less money, which makes it unaffordable for many workers. Some claim it will reduce productivity and lead to economic failure.

Will a shorter working week mean that people can't choose?

Under some manifestations of capitalism, interfering with personal choice is a cardinal offence against free market functioning. But no choice is made in a vacuum. It is shaped by the cultures, norms and incentives that surround us. Our proposal is to disrupt and influence these determinants, and establish new standards for the expected time anyone should work over a week, month or year. Individuals would continue to choose, but within a different set of parameters.

We readily acknowledge that the shift is likely to start on a piecemeal and voluntary basis – it already has. But relying on free choice alone within the unreformed structures of today's economy is not our goal – for at least three reasons.

First, reduced hours are currently most often 'chosen' by women with domestic responsibilities. Like ideas about a 'normal' working week, most of our choices are socially and economically constructed. Some of us are much freer to choose than others. As we have seen, women traditionally take on caring and other domestic responsibilities, and therefore have little option but to go for 'part-time' or intermittent jobs, while men, as higher earners, carry on working longer hours – and so the pattern of gender inequality is perpetuated.

Second, in a world where reduced working time is merely an option, it is likely to be 'chosen' more often by better-paid workers who feel they can afford to do so – deepening inequalities between those who are affluent in time as well as money, and those who are not. To counteract this problem, we argue that it is also essential to improve pay and conditions for lower income groups (see below). But that won't be enough on its own. The ultimate goal is sufficient work and sufficient income for all – men and women, higher and lower paid – and a new standard working week closer to four days (or its equivalent in annual hours), achievable for everyone on equal terms.

Third, in a competitive setting, people often feel their job depends on demonstrating commitment through working well beyond paid-for hours. In this case, enthusiasm for work (like choice) is more constructed than spontaneous, less a matter of freedom than of necessity and/or ambition.

If reduced working time simply remains an option within the current economic system, these patterns will intensify. What we need, then, is a careful balance between establishing statutory limits for all and enabling customized pathways to work-time reduction. Within a strategy that reduces average working hours overall, there is plenty of room for flexibility in how work time is allocated. But workers themselves must have enough power to arrange working hours to suit their own needs.

Some Challenges

Is leisure more sustainable?

As we have noted, one reason for reduced working time is to make it easier for people to live more sustainably. It can free up time for caring, for example, which is a low-carbon activity. Having more free time can discourage 'convenience' shopping and energy-intensive travel, and encourage more resource-neutral behaviour.

But how many of us use leisure time in a sustainable way? There's a strong link here with relatively unsustainable patterns of consumption among higher income groups. Better-off people are more likely to spend a three-day weekend jetting off to a 'city break' or a ski resort. Walking in the countryside is undoubtedly a sustainable way of spending time, but not if you fly to Patagonia or Portugal to do so.

And then there are hobbies such as bird-watching. This can start with zero-carbon keen-sightedness in the back garden or local park. Then you buy binoculars and a camera – relatively harmless, but nevertheless involving energy and resources in manufacture. You might soon feel inspired to buy a tripod, a zoom lens, all-weather clothing, a sophisticated tent, and move on from travelling by train to nature reserves to investing in an SUV that will carry you to more distant and enviable bird-watching sites. Once you become a serious twitcher,[1] you may drive thousands of miles a year or even leap on planes to spot rare birds in exotic locations before they depart. Thus, the simple nature-lover morphs into a rapacious pleasure-seeker with a hefty ecological footprint. As Nicholas Milton of the UK's Royal Society for the Protection of Birds (RSPB) has warned, 'if most of the RSPB's million-plus members suddenly gave up being garden bird spotters and instead became twitchers it would be a climate catastrophe.'[2]

How we spend our leisure hours depends on generalized norms about consumption habits, how we develop our interests and priorities, what we know, who our friends are, what opportunities are available to us and how much money we have at our disposal. On balance, reduced working time is likely to have more positive than negative impacts on the environment in the medium to longer term – both by shifting the cultural focus of reward from income to time, and by helping to change consumption habits associated with 'convenience'. But it must go hand-in-hand with other policies to deter environmentally damaging behaviours and to foster sustainable living.

Some Challenges

What about pay?

Today's culture of long-hours working is reinforced by rates of pay, with national minima kept to a level where survival depends on a five-day week or more. From October 2020, the UK's minimum wage was £8.72 per hour for adults over the age of 25. If you worked at this rate for 30 hours a week for all 52 weeks in a year, you would end up with gross pay of around £13,600. You'd have to work more than 67 hours a week – with only two weeks off – to reach the national median annual earnings.[3] For many working people, unsurprisingly, the biggest worry about reduced working time is loss of income.

The main problem is low hourly rates of pay. No one should have to work over-long hours – with all the well-documented risks to health and wellbeing – in order to make ends meet. Moving to reduced hours must be accompanied by measures to ensure that everyone is entitled to a real living wage, which must be shifted towards a level that is sufficient for a shorter working week (we return to this in Chapter 5). And at the same time, we should aim for an enhanced and secure 'social income', in the form of more and better public services that are available to all according to need, not ability to pay.[4] This social income has a redistributive effect and supplements earned income.[5]

So the prospect of casting people into poverty is a good reason to fight for better hourly rates of pay and public services. It is a poor stand-alone reason for objecting to a shorter working week. But what of all those who are a long way from poverty, but would nonetheless fear a loss of income from reduced hours?

What matters is how we make the transition to a shorter working week. For a start, we propose gradually increasing a blend of different statutory entitlements to time off for all, with protected pay. Examples include extended parental leave, new entitlements to care leave, longer statutory annual leave, additional one-day national holidays, flexibility to taper retirement and the right to negotiate reduced hours. Taken together with significant increases in the minimum wage, this would build experience of cutting hours without losing pay, for employers as well as workers, building confidence in the process of moving towards a new 'normal' and enabling the economy to adjust.

As part of the transition, alongside regulatory measures, a gradual shift can be negotiated at sector or workplace level. For example, as Juliet Schor suggests,[6] in organizations where there is an annual pay review and settlement, workers could trade a bit more time off for a bit less in pay growth each year. Everyone would get a smaller pay increment and gain additional minutes or hours of disposable time away from the workplace. Year on year, the workforce would steadily shorten their working week and no one would experience an immediate pay cut.

This approach won't work everywhere (it's better suited to larger organizations and to workers who are already on good earnings). But the more widely it is adopted, the more it will help to build experience of reduced working time, and to change prevailing attitudes about how work should be rewarded, what is meant by 'success' and what constitutes a flourishing life.

Is a shorter working week bad for the economy?

It is often claimed that reduced working time threatens to reduce output and is therefore incompatible with efforts to build a thriving economy. In any case, it is argued, productivity must first rise significantly in order to facilitate any further reduction in hours.

Robert Skidelsky points to a dynamic relationship

between working hours and productivity: 'Falling hours are associated with high measured productivity growth; high productivity growth with high investment ratios and rising real wages; and rising real wages with shorter working hours.' As we have seen, the length of the working week in industrialized countries has almost halved over the last 150 years. The downward trend continued until the 1980s and then stopped falling, albeit with notable variations.[7] More recently, productivity growth has flat-lined in many industrialized countries, while wages have struggled to rise in line with inflation. It is therefore argued (in some quarters) that reduced working time has become *unachievable* because productivity is falling and *undesirable* because it is likely to have a negative impact on output. How are we to deal with this double-edged challenge?

Will automation come to the rescue?

One view is that we are in the throes of a new 'industrial revolution', with developments in robotics, communications and artificial intelligence that promise to boost productivity and at the same time reduce demand for human labour.[8] Accordingly, this will create a fresh set of favourable conditions for a shorter working week. What's more, new technologies are less dependent on fossil fuels and generally cleaner and greener than their predecessors, so we can worry less (it is claimed) about rising levels of GHG emissions or depletion of natural resources[9] – which are manifestly catastrophic consequences of earlier productivity growth. Optimists of this tendency envisage investment in technologies that are 'weightless' in terms of energy and resource use, enabling organizations to shift to shorter hours, resulting in a contented and well-rewarded workforce contributing to robust productivity within a shrinking ecological footprint.

It sounds good, but things are a lot more complicated in real life. As we noted earlier, automation will affect different sectors of the economy unevenly, probably with a polarizing effect that widens inequalities. In any case, rising productivity alone, regardless of whether it is facilitated by automation, will not guarantee better wages for workers, less inequality in income and wealth or a more sustainable economy. What counts is where power lies and how it is deployed. A critical factor in cutting hours of work in the twentieth century was collective bargaining, which enabled workers to win a share of productivity gains. Trade union power has declined dramatically since the 1980s and, more recently, the rise of digital platforms has made it harder to organize workers effectively.

Some Challenges

It is far from certain that cleaner and greener technologies alone will prevent the breaching of ecological boundaries that threatens the future of the planet. If new technologies boost output, we can expect higher profits for businesses, bigger dividends for shareholders and sometimes also better pay for workers. In the absence of shifts in the nature of consumption, and in prevailing expectations that reward must take the form of ever higher personal incomes, it is most unlikely that any technological breakthrough will make the economy ecologically sustainable. Even if we did manage to techno-fix our way out of climate crisis, we would still run a high risk of breaching other planetary boundaries such as biodiversity in the process.

The technophile optimists' vision could only be realized in some organizations, for some groups of workers, in some sectors, influencing a small portion of the economy. It would be futile to imagine it could be scaled up to transform the economy as a whole. What's required alongside technological change is a massive shift towards renewable energy and circular resource use, to transform patterns of consumption and reshape the meaning and purpose of economic activity.

Can rising hour-for-hour productivity compensate for lost time?

When it is claimed that reduced working time is bad for business, it is usually on the basis that it will reduce output. Against this, it is argued that workers who put in fewer hours tend to be more productive for each hour worked. What often happens is that people working eight hours or more per day get tired towards the end of the shift and perform less well. The more hours they work, the greater the risk of stress and anxiety, which can also make them less productive. As a rule, workers and workplaces also tend to prioritize. This means that, when people move to shorter hours, the tasks that are sacrificed first tend to be less important, and invariably less productive. At the same time, cutting hours can help workers stay in better health, take fewer days off, be more alert and focused at work and even feel more committed to the employer: all of which can help to improve output through higher hour-for-hour productivity. This is borne out by the experience of Gothenburg's Toyota service centre (see pp. 17–18) as well as by many other employers, ranging from US car plants in 1932 to New Zealand financial services in 2018 (see pp. 86–9). A 2019 UK survey found that 74 per cent of workers said they could finish a week's work in four days.[10] And, as we have noted, countries with lower average working hours tend to have higher levels of GDP.

However, this doesn't work in all sectors of the economy. Tim Jackson identifies three kinds of work, 'care, craft and culture', that challenge conventional notions about what amounts to productivity. Here, human relationships, creativity and generous expenditure of time determine the quality of a job done, rather than the speed or the volume of output per hour worked. As Jackson observes, the care and concern of one human being for another cannot be stockpiled and is not deliverable by machines. New technologies can and do help, but 'cannot ultimately substitute for the time spent by caregivers'. Similarly, 'it is the accuracy and detail inherent in crafted goods that endow them with lasting value', not the quantity produced in a fixed period of time. Cultural endeavours, says Jackson, 'generally tend to resist the logic of labour productivity because their vital ingredient is the time and skill of the artist.'[11] In short, there are some jobs where the value of what is produced is more likely to increase if workers put in more, rather than less, time. Output per hour worked is either irrelevant to the job, or unmeasurable, or both.

Across all sectors, some companies are bound to struggle with reduced working hours and may even go out of business. However, if weekly wages can be maintained as far as possible during early policy interventions that increase time off, then overall spending in the economy can also be maintained. Protecting aggregate demand in the short term will enable other companies to thrive and expand recruitment, avoiding immediate shocks to the economy that could otherwise jeopardize progress towards social and environmental goals.

We are not aiming to reduce working time regardless of the consequences, but in order to improve wellbeing, reduce inequalities and safeguard the natural environment. Rising productivity will compensate for lost working time in some sectors but not in others. Even where it does, there remains the challenge of bringing the nature of output and consumption into line with ecological sustainability.

What about the 24/7 economy?
How much of a threat would reduced working time pose to an increasingly prominent feature of today's economy – namely, the demand for 24/7 work regimes? Healthcare is an obvious example, but there are also large swathes of the service and manufacturing sectors where long hours or round-the-clock shifts are either integral to the purpose of the work, or necessary to justify investment,

or have become what customers expect. In some sectors, shorter shifts and higher rates of hour-for-hour productivity should be able to meet the need to be 'always on' without significant extra cost. In others, such as healthcare, there would have to be additional recruitment, which would cost employers more. There would be gains in terms of reduced sick leave and absenteeism, a healthier and more committed workforce, and probably also better quality of work. There would also be fewer people unemployed with all the attendant risks we noted earlier. Some, but not all, of these gains would accrue to the employer. There remains a role for governments, where appropriate, to coordinate action in areas such as healthcare where the public interest is at stake. Some parts of the 24/7 economy may be considered ecologically unsustainable in the longer term.

Rethinking the goals of the economy

Our answer to the question 'Is a shorter working week bad for the economy?' is that it depends what is meant by 'bad'. We must change the way economic success is measured.

The narrow metric of GDP tells us very little about

how well the economy is performing in terms of its impact on society and the natural environment. It is a measure of the market value of all goods and services produced and sold for a monetary value. It tells us about some economic activities, but nothing about the source of them – for example, whether they come from fracking or investment in green energy technologies, from gambling or social care. Even the inventor of GDP, Simon Kuznets, was concerned about this. He urged that distinctions 'be kept in mind between quantity and quality of growth, between its costs and return, and between the short and the long term. Goals for more growth should specify more growth of what and for what.'[12]

Put another way, what's 'bad' or 'good' for the economy is a matter of judgement that evolves over time, not a fixed, scientific fact. Tim Jackson argues that the 'task of the economy is to deliver and to enable prosperity. But prosperity is not synonymous with material wealth and its requirements go beyond material sustenance'; it is about our ability to flourish physically, psychologically and socially, and 'to participate meaningfully in the life of society'.[13]

Studies in the US have found that young Americans today are more likely to have slightly less happiness and much greater risk of depression and assorted social pathologies than their grand-parents, despite having grown up with considerable affluence: becoming 'better off over the last four decades has not been accompanied by one iota of increased subjective well-being'.[14]

The New Economics Foundation has long argued that the health of a country's economy cannot be measured in terms of productivity or GDP alone. NEF developed the case for measuring wellbeing, as a nuanced concept that includes how satisfied people are with their lives as a whole, as well as factors such as autonomy and purpose.[15] It pioneered the Happy Planet Index, which combines measures of wellbeing, life expectancy, inequality and ecological footprint to provide a rudimentary comparison of 'how efficiently residents of different countries are using environmental resources to lead long, happy lives'.[16]

While the OECD now measures wellbeing on an annual basis,[17] the goal of economic 'growth' measured solely in terms of GDP is still uncritically promulgated by most governments and mainstream institutions. In her book *Doughnut Economics*, Kate Raworth takes issue with this. She makes the case for measuring 'an ecologically safe and socially just space for humanity' between an inner limit defined by shortfalls in 'life's essentials such as food, education and housing' and an outer limit defined by overshooting planetary boundaries, including climate change, resource depletion, biodiversity loss, and pollution. What's good for the economy, she says, is not 'endless GDP growth', but 'thriving-in-balance' within these social and ecological boundaries.[18]

Our case for a shorter working week is based on evidence that it contributes to human flourishing and social participation within ecological limits. The goal of 'thriving-in-balance' cannot be measured in terms of GDP. Striving for more productivity is a worthwhile objective only if it leads to prosperity with fairer and more sustainable outcomes.

Taking all this into account, we can envisage a new momentum towards a shorter working week. Not just technological wizardry, but a redistribution of work and time. Not just endless consumption and accumulation, but a renewed quest for human flourishing. In place of exhausting and exploitative long-hours working, more jobs for more people in conditions that are conducive to wellbeing, social justice, and a sustainable future.

4

Learning from Practical Experience

We have drawn inspiration from a great many practical initiatives to reduce working time. These come in all shapes and sizes, and over the course of two centuries. They have involved a variety of strategies, ranging from nationwide rules laid down by government and regulations enabling individuals to choose, to sectoral agreements negotiated by trade unions and ad hoc arrangements at company level. We have already noted some of them, including Roosevelt's bid to persuade US employers to move to 35 hours in 1933 and Toyota's introduction of six-hour shifts in Gothenburg, Sweden, in 2002. Here we take a closer look at a selection of initiatives that illustrate different approaches. Since history, culture and politics play an important role in shaping the 'normal' allocation of paid hours, what works in one setting may not work in another.

61

In any event, there are useful lessons that we draw together at the end of the chapter.

We start with interventions by national and local governments, then consider trade union negotiations, initiatives by individual employers and a national campaign coalition.

State-led interventions

Governments are sometimes moved to cut hours of work in times of economic crises. Roosevelt did so during the Great Recession. In the UK in 1974, in the face of sharply rising oil prices and an imminent strike by coalminers, Edward Heath's Conservative government introduced a three-day week from January to March, to conserve fuel supplies. The French government was facing an acute unemployment problem when it cut the working week in 1998. Most recently, the 2020 COVID-19 crisis provoked new interest in shorter and more flexible hours as governments attempted to reboot their economies and get people back to work. Yet it is not always a matter of crisis management, as we shall see.

Government interventions set out here include national legislation to install a shorter working week in France, local state initiatives in Sweden and the US to cut hours for particular groups of workers, and national provisions that enable individuals to choose to reduce their hours in the Netherlands and Belgium.

A 35-hour week in France

Between 1998 and 2001, the French government passed groundbreaking legislation to cut the standard working week from 39 to 35 hours. France was then – and remains – the only country to have used national legislation as the primary means of cutting hours across the workforce.

The move followed years of debate about the virtues of reducing working time to make room for political activities and for family and personal development.[1] But what ultimately drove the government to take action was the rate of unemployment, which had reached 12.5 per cent. Socialist prime minister Lionel Jospin, in coalition with the Greens and Communists, took the view that reduced hours would help to share available work by creating more jobs.

It was a complex and ambitious policy, which not only aimed to reduce working time but also restructured French labour law and triggered an expansion of workplace bargaining. These changes are said to have affected 'job creation, productivity, labour relations and working conditions, possibly more than the average hours worked'.[2]

The legislation, in two parts and named after then Minister of Social Affairs Martine Aubry (Aubry 1 and 2), combined statutory reduction of hours with active encouragement for trade unions and employers to negotiate ways of achieving the 35-hour goal at local level. Employers were given financial incentives to cut hours and create new jobs within a two-year deadline. There was a parallel reduction in tax contributions (especially for lower wages) and an eighteen-month wage freeze.[3]

The measures were presented as a way of improving company performance by increasing work-time flexibility. While the public sector was exempt from both laws, government bodies applied the 35-hour limit to a majority of their workers.[4]

By 1998, the 35-hour working week had been adopted by 30,000 companies employing 2 million workers.[5] Some 350,000 new jobs were created, although this may be attributed more to reduced payroll taxes than to reduced hours, and to a turn in the economic tide, which ushered in a new era of rapid growth. Opposition to the 35-hour week was strong among employers and politicians on the right. Partly in response, the second Aubry law, passed in 2000, instituted a new legal norm of 1,600 hours per year, which allowed employers to impose flexible schedules over which workers had little or no control.

When the socialist coalition lost the 2002 elections to the centre-right, incoming president Nicolas Sarkozy vowed to end mandatory reduced working time, replacing the socialists' mantra of 'work less to live better' with 'work more to earn more'. From that point, various aspects of the Aubry laws were dismantled. Estimates vary as to how far working time was actually reduced. Figure 2 shows a significant drop around the turn of the decade, with average hours in France comparable to those in the UK, but well below those in the USA and the OECD average.

How the legislation was implemented differed between companies, locations and sectors, because of local negotiations and multiple exemptions. As time went by and new legislation chipped away at the Aubry laws, it became increasingly apparent that hours were unequally distributed. While there was a net reduction of roughly two hours per week for blue-collar and clerical workers between 1997 and 2008, there was found to be 'no observable reduction effect for high-skilled employees in the same period'.[6] Overall, men experienced a greater

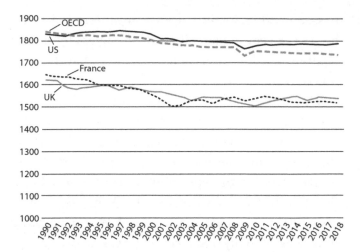

Figure 2: Average annual hours actually worked per worker, 1990–2018, selected countries and OECD average.

Source: OECD https://stats.oecd.org/Index.aspx?DataSetCode=AVE_HRS

reduction in hours than women, although this was largely due to many women opting to shift from part-time work to 35 hours, a move attributed to France's 'highly developed public childcare and pre-school services'.[7]

Among workers whose hours had been reduced by the Aubry legislation, well over half responded positively when asked if it had made it easier to combine family and working life. This held true for different types of work and salary levels, and for men as well as for women.[8] The 35-hour week was most consistently popular among parents of young children.

Workplace agreements suited some workers better than others. In firms where there was already a positive attitude to work–life balance, workers found the reduction in hours to be more beneficial – possibly because employers were more willing to realize the purpose, rather than just the letter, of the law. Elsewhere, however, many found that their work intensified, especially where additional workers were not recruited, and this made their lives more stressful. In the wake of the second Aubry law, people found they had less control over their working time, which had a negative impact on the quality of their lives. This loss of control eroded support among workers for reduced hours.

A more positive effect was that newly mobilized structures for collective bargaining tended to impede attempts to roll back the laws after 2002. The fact that the Aubry legislation had promoted local agreements meant that a great many workplace organizations negotiated reduced working hours – and in doing so developed a sense of investment in them.

For all Sarkozy's efforts, and in spite of cooling

enthusiasm on the political left, the 35-hour week has not actually been abolished. It is still officially the 'norm', adhered to by many French employers and workers, although more now work longer hours. It has been estimated that, between 1998 and 2008, 'the overall net effect of the statutory 35-hour limit amounted to roughly 1.5 hours per week'. This was well below the original goal, but 'the largest drop in Western Europe in this time period'.[9] French workers currently put in fewer hours per year on average than all but four OECD countries (Germany, Norway, Denmark and the Netherlands).

A six-hour day trial for care workers in Gothenburg, Sweden

An old people's nursing home in Gothenburg, Sweden's second largest city, was the site of a much-publicized experiment from 2015 to 2017. This was a temporary trial, introduced by the city government and subject to a controlled evaluation. At the Svartedalen home, 68 care staff had been on a standard eight-hour day and were moved to a six-hour day with no loss of pay; 17 extra staff were recruited to make up the extra time. Costs were covered by public funds.

Sweden has a large and rapidly growing population of 80-year-olds and over, and healthcare workers (predominantly female) are often obliged to undertake gruelling shifts with significant repercussions on their health and performance at work. The city council wanted to find out if reduced working time would improve workers' wellbeing as well as the quality of care they gave to residents.

Evaluators compared Svartedalen with Solangen, a similar facility, which retained a 39-hour week. They found that more staff at Svartedalen reported significant health gains than staff in the control group, as well as greater alertness, less stress and a more active lifestyle. They slept better, had lower blood pressure and were absent less often through sickness. The residents at Svartedalen reported more positive experiences, as staff did more activities with them, such as walking in the open air, singing and dancing.

Monica Axhede, director of the Svartedalen home, said she found the atmosphere became more relaxed: 'We have many people here who suffer from dementia. Before, when there was too much stress around, it made them very nervous. Now they are clearly more peaceful.'[10] Daniel Bernmar, Gothenburg city councillor, observed: 'Day-to-day interaction improved when the staff were less stressed. The guests and the staff were more engaged. We measured the amount of daily activities organized for our guests and we found them to have risen by 60 per cent. The number of sick leave days plummeted, too.'[11]

Councillor Bernmar took the view that, if the approach were implemented widely, it could have an 'extremely positive' fiscal impact. 'Hiring more people means lower unemployment, for example, which is a social cost. Shortening work shifts and making them less stressful leads to fewer cases of sick leave, which translates into a smaller burden on the healthcare system.' Although hiring extra staff would drive up costs by 20–30 per cent, Bernmar said, 'in the long run, it drives down collateral costs associated with unemployment and healthcare by 15 per cent'.[12]

While the experiment was a success on many levels, it was ultimately scuppered by politics and price tag. It cost the equivalent of €12 million and came in on budget, but by the time it was over the left coalition had lost control of the city council and a majority was formed by right-wing parties that had fiercely opposed the trial from the start. The incoming deputy mayor said she feared that if all the city's 530,000 employees worked six hours for eight hours' pay, the cost would be prohibitive. 'We need more hands, we need more people to go to work, and we even need to work longer.' In addition, the LO, Sweden's trade union confederation, had other priorities – getting more people into traditional 'full-time' jobs.

Findings from Svartedalen echo those from earlier trials in Sweden. For example, the Swedish National Institute of Working Life ran an eighteen-month randomized control led trial of the impact of reduced working hours, without loss of pay, in randomly selected workplaces across four sectors (social services, technical services, care and welfare, and call centres). In the intervention group, workers' daily hours were reduced from eight to six, and employers received funding to recruit more staff; the workers agreed not to carry out extra paid work in their free time and filled in diaries throughout the trial. Across all sectors in this experiment, workers with reduced hours reported greater quality of sleep, lower daytime tiredness and reduced stress (in particular, reduced worry and stress at bedtime).[13]

A compressed working week in Utah, USA
In 2008, the state government in Utah launched a bold expriment, affecting employees in most state services. At only a month's notice, 18,000 of the state's 25,000 workforce were put on a four-day

week with a three-day weekend. Hours per week stayed the same, with a new compressed schedule running from 7 a.m. to 6 p.m. Around 900 public buildings closed on Fridays, with extended hours from Monday to Thursday.

High fuel costs had triggered the initiative, but its stated purpose was more ambitious: 'To make a positive impact in the areas of energy consumption, extended customer service, employee recruitment and retention, and reducing the environmental impact of state government operations.'[14] The compressed schedule was compulsory for all workers, except those in agencies delivering emergency and public safety services, prisons and public universities.

This version of a four-day week was not new to the US. More than one in three organizations have offered compressed working along similar lines, most commonly with four 10-hour days and either Friday or Monday off.[15] The Utah experiment was unique in its scope, ambition and mandatory nature. It was also closely studied from the outset until it was wound up in 2011.

Research into the effects was hampered by unanticipated factors – including a fall in the price of fuel, a new highway that affected commuting patterns, warming temperatures that reduced heating costs and fallout from the 2008 financial crisis.

Nevertheless the experiment produced some useful findings.

The scheme was popular with employees. While just over half said before the experiment started that they would prefer the four-day schedule, nearly three-quarters said they preferred it once they had experienced it in practice. There were lower rates of overtime, and less absenteeism and sick leave. Some parents reported problems fitting in with after-school and childcare routines, but most said they preferred the new schedule. They were saving money on commuting costs, found roads less crowded when travelling to and from work and appreciated time to do local voluntary activities on Fridays. In the end, 82 per cent said they wanted the pilot to continue.

The four-day week also found favour with users of the state services. More than two-thirds of those surveyed wanted the pilot to continue, compared with 20 per cent who wanted it to stop. More than 70 per cent found that services were sufficient to meet their needs and nearly 80 per cent reported that the four-day week had made no difference to them. Use of online services continued to increase.[16]

Fuel consumption and CO_2 production by vehicles in the public fleet fell by 2 per cent and 14 per cent respectively, although there is no account of how the scheme affected private fuel consumption or GHG emissions.[17] Energy consumed by public buildings was reduced by 10.5 per cent, leading to annual savings of $502,000, while operation costs fell by $203,000.[18] However, while it had been hoped that closing some state buildings on Fridays would lead to annual savings of about $3 million, the final tally was closer to $1 million.[19]

As in Sweden, it was in the end politics and price that undermined the four-day week. Jon Huntsman, the Utah state governor who had championed it initially, left office in 2009 to become ambassador to China. When the state legislature ended the experiment in 2011, the narrative changed. According to the representative who sponsored the closure bill, 'the biggest concerns came from people who had to access services on Friday. The business community didn't like it, and the court system didn't like it at all. ... The whole idea, it just didn't work very well.'[20]

Voluntary reductions in the Netherlands
Governments in the Netherlands have not tried to cut weekly hours across the workforce, but have focused instead on measures to support individual choice, aiming in particular to get more women into paid work. A 1985 'Policy Plan for Emancipation'

officially acknowledged that economic independence was a necessary condition for women's emancipation. As more women entered the labour market, demands grew for measures that would make it easier to combine paid work with the care of young children. Measures to extend childcare and parental leave between 1988 and 1991 were followed by the Working Hours Act, which came into force in 1995. This obliged employers to take account of employees' personal circumstances when stipulating hours of work and break times. It also allowed for collective agreements to regulate working time, including leave for breast-feeding, working at home and flexible arrangements that distributed working time across a day, week or month.

Five years later, the Working Hours Adjustment Act obliged employers to agree to workers' requests to reduce working hours 'for the purpose of enabling a better combination of paid work and care tasks' unless there were compelling management or business reasons not to do so. This was followed by the Work and Care Act 2001, which consolidated and strengthened measures to reconcile care and paid employment. Importantly, the Act recognized that this was no longer a matter of personal responsibility given the overriding public interest in female emancipation and participation in the labour force (which mattered most is an interesting question, but beyond the scope of this discussion).

Further measures ensued over the next decade, establishing a legal right to long-term care leave, a parental leave tax credit to provide some financial compensation, a doubling of parental leave and a wider range of purposes for which leave can be taken. In 2010, maximum hours were set at 48 hours per week averaged over a 16-week period, with no single week longer than 60 hours. In 2017 the Flexible Working Act came into force, which enabled workers to request changes not only to their working hours, but also to their work location (although employers were not obliged to agree to the latter). They could make their requests within shorter timeframes than previous legislation had allowed. As these regulations developed, there was continuing provision for collective bargaining to settle detailed arrangements locally.

Many more women and highly paid workers have opted for reduced hours than have men or lower-paid workers. While there are some minimal arrangements for financial compensation, cutting hours usually means cutting income. In 2006, the Dutch government introduced a Life-Course Saving Scheme that offered tax breaks for those who put up to 12 per cent of their salary aside to help finance unpaid leave in the future. But the scheme was poorly designed, and take-up remained low until it was closed to new users in 2012 and effectively wound up.

Time credits in Belgium

The Belgian Time Credit Scheme, introduced in 2002, gives workers in the private sector the right to take a break at any stage of their working lives, for any purpose. (Public sector workers have their own career break arrangements that are similar.) Like the Dutch scheme, it supports voluntary time reduction, but takes a different approach, with more explicit emphasis on promoting better quality of life and some compensation for loss of pay.

Individuals can choose to take up to a year of full-time leave, or to cut their hours in half for up to two years, or to reduce them by 20 per cent for up to five years, in one or more blocks. The right to opt for a career break depends on having worked for the employer for a specified minimum period. Only 5 per cent of employees in an organization can take leave under the scheme at any one time. Those who opt for a break get a small flat rate benefit paid out of unemployment insurance funds, and the rate varies according to their age, what type of break they choose and how long they have worked for the employer. They have a right to get their job back at the end of the break. There are additional three-month, one-off breaks, specifically for childcare, medical and palliative care, which include higher levels of benefit.[21]

An earlier career break system founded in 1985 aimed primarily to get more people into paid work and obliged employers to replace each worker who took a break with someone entitled to unemployment benefit. It was more limited in scope and did not include any guaranteed return to work. The Time Credit Scheme gives more weight to life beyond the workplace and has removed the obligation to replace staff on leave. The fact that it was introduced by the Law on Reconciliation of Employment and Quality of Life has been heralded as an important signal that the goal of a better work–life balance is embedded in the nation's legal framework, reflecting what has been described as a 'strong collective solidarity logic'.[22]

Time credits are popular with workers and quite widely used. On the plus side, the scheme is flexible, in that it enables those who qualify to take leave for any purpose they choose, and at any time during their working lives; it is rights-based and it ensures that breaks are covered by small, but not insignificant, benefit payments.

On the minus side, there are few signs that time credits are helping to promote greater equality. There is far higher take-up among men than under the earlier career break system, but they appear to take breaks for reasons that have little to do with sharing domestic responsibilities. While most women take career breaks in their 20s and 30s, most men take them later in life, apparently as a step towards early retirement.[23] As for income inequalities, the benefits that accompany time credits may make it easier for low-income workers to participate (compared with the Dutch scheme), but the criteria for entry remain a barrier. The more disadvantaged workers are more likely to be in short-term precarious jobs and are therefore less able to build up a suitable employment record.

The scheme has been popular with employees, but less so with employers, largely for management reasons, or with government, because of mounting costs. The fiscal implications of high take-up have prompted discussions about whether time credits should be replaced by a time-saving scheme along the lines of the German working time accounts (see below), or by a wage-saving arrangement similar to the Dutch Life-Course Saving Scheme. Each of these would shift costs from the public purse to individual workers, excluding the more disadvantaged and widening gender and income inequalities. So far, the Time Credit Scheme has not been superseded by any alternative, perhaps because its flaws have not yet been found to outweigh its strengths.

Negotiated agreements at sector and workplace levels

For trade unions, negotiating shorter hours is often a means of avoiding lay-offs, especially in times of economic downturn. But a strong and enduring motivation has been for social progress: to enable workers 'to live healthy, dignified, and high-quality lives'. In the last half-century there has been an increasingly strong emphasis on reconciling paid employment and family responsibilities, often described as 'work–life balance'. As the French experience shows, national legislation and work-place-level agreements can complement each other. Here we consider the role of unions in Germany and the UK, where negotiated settlements have been the main driver of reduced working time.

Negotiated settlements in Germany
Trade unions in Germany have long played a powerful role in negotiating with employers for pay

and conditions, including reduced working time. In 1953, the largest of them, IG Metall (IGM), the metal-workers' union, negotiated a settlement at one factory for a 40-hour week with no loss of pay. It subsequently won paid vacation time and sick leave for members and began to campaign for a 35-hour week. This was done with a view to 'humanizing the workplace' as well as safeguarding jobs in the wake of the 1973 oil crisis.[24] After a seven-week strike in 1984, IGM secured a 35-hour week for workers in Baden-Württemberg and Hesse. The settlement put working time reduction on the table as an achievable goal.[25] Negotiations spread to other industries and confirmed Germany as a leading exemplar of a successful economy with relatively low average working hours.

Trade union power began to decline from the mid-1980s, due to shifts in global politics and trade as well as to German reunification in 1990. The proportion of workers who were unionized fell from 34.7 to 19.9 per cent over two decades.[26] Meanwhile, employers were exploring the benefits of combining reduced hours with flexible working as a way of coping with fluctuating demand.

In 1993, IGM negotiated a landmark deal with Volkswagen that reduced the working week by 20 per cent, from 36 to 28.8 hours per week. This avoided mass lay-offs, but resulted in some loss of pay and benefits for employees, as well as more flexible and less predictable working arrangements. Hours were annualized and a system of time-banking was introduced. By 1999, the threat of redundancies had all but disappeared and most employees went back to longer hours. In 2006, the company returned officially to a 33-hour and 34-hour week for blue-collar and white-collar workers respectively.[27]

The time-banking system, known as 'working-time accounts', became increasingly common. These allowed for hours to be stored and redeemed over an agreed period, with spells of reduced time traded for longer hours at a later date (and vice versa). From the mid-1990s, flexible working became the norm in the metal-working industry and, by 2000, 78 per cent of private sector employers offered workers some form of working time account.[28] The structure of these accounts varied widely, as did the extent to which workers could control how their time was managed.

After the financial crisis of 2008, IGM began to rebuild its membership, with new tactics to appeal to younger members and a focus on local organizing. Between 2010 and 2015, its in-work membership soared by 94,000. In 2018, after six rounds of often bruising talks and a series of 24-hour strikes in more than eighty companies, IGM struck a deal with the Südwestmetall employers' organization that gave nearly a million workers not only a 4.3 per cent pay rise, but also the option of a 28-hour week for up to two years, with a right to return to full-time employment.

It was not a threat of mass redundancies that propelled the parties to a deal in this case, but a growing interest among employees in achieving a better work–life balance. As one union member with a pre-school child commented, 'it's always nice to have a bit of extra cash in your pocket, but for me the core win the union managed to gain was the new work-time model.'[29] Workers who took up the option in order to care for young children or ageing parents received an additional allowance, while those wanting a break from shift work with a high health risk would be compensated with €750 per year.[30]

A survey of union members found that a majority favoured temporary work-time reductions and greater personal flexibility in order to 'harmonize job requirements with their private lives', while a significant minority supported a general reduction in hours, even 'if this meant a cut in payment gains'.[31] The deal reportedly reflected a new mind-set among younger workers. *Handelsblatt*, a business newspaper, called it 'the credo of the new age: that time is more valuable than money'. Hanna Schwander, public policy professor at Berlin's Hertie School of Governance, told the London *Financial Times* that 'more and more people have periods in their lives when they want to work less, for example to look after elderly relatives, or to take a sabbatical or unpaid leave'. And IGM chairman Jörg Hofmann called the 28-hour deal 'a milestone on the path to a modern, self-determined world of work'.[32]

Settlements by IGM have tended to blaze a trail for other sectors. Postal and transport workers, for example, have pursued negotiations for more time off. Whether the trend will outlast Germany's economic boom is a matter for speculation.

'Drive for 35', UK Communication Workers Union

When the UK Communication Workers Union (CWU) launched its 'Drive for 35', it did so in response to automation, although in this case the primary goal was to safeguard members' wellbeing, rather than to avoid lay-offs. In 2015, Royal Mail introduced a new system that began automating large numbers of parcel-sorting jobs. As a result, the amount of time postal workers spent on delivery rounds increased from four to seven hours. Their average age was 49 years and they claimed that having to push around heavy loads for seven hours a day would pose a serious risk to their health. In 2016, the CWU adopted a policy aiming to achieve a 35-hour gross basic working week by 2020, with no reduction in pay. It cited 'a significant body of independent research that indicates that a shorter working week, linked to improvements in working practices and organization, led to people being able to work better and more effectively while reducing fatigue'. It pledged to use this evidence in talks with Royal Mail.[33]

In 2018, the union reached an agreement with the Royal Mail Group (RMG) for an incremental transition to a 35-hour week by 2022. This was hailed as the greatest negotiated decrease in weekly working hours in the UK since engineering unions moved from 39 to 37.5 hours in the 1990s. Reducing hours for full-time workers would help address key issues for the business and its employees, said the union. These included 'automation, resourcing, workloads, overtime and part-time employment' as well as a commitment to having 'a predominately full-time workforce'.[34]

A joint statement from the CWU and the Royal Mail Group announced that the first one-hour reduction in the working week would commence in

October 2018. The second one-hour reduction was due a year later, but RMG did not follow through. The CWU balloted for strike action in support of the 'four pillars' – shorter working week, pensions, a redesigned operational pipeline and extended legal protections. Members voted overwhelmingly in favour, but the RMG sought and gained a high court injunction against strike action in November 2019. Dave Ward, CWU General Secretary, said his members were 'extremely angry and bitterly disappointed' with the judgment and vowed that RMG's victory would be 'short-lived'.[35]

Employers' initiatives

There are countless examples of employers taking the initiative to reduce working time – too many to document here. Almost invariably they do so to improve the company's performance. Here are two examples.

A four-day week at Perpetual Guardian, New Zealand

The New Zealand financial services company Perpetual Guardian has been one of the first major private sector employers to introduce a four-day week without loss of pay. The company launched an eight-week trial in the spring of 2018, switching all 240 staff from a five-day, 37.5-hour week to a four-day, 30-hour week, with individuals' days off decided at team level. Workers were expected to maintain the same levels of output as they had on a five-day week. Company founder Andrew Barnes said he was inspired by reports in *The Economist* that workers in the UK and Canada put in fewer than three hours of productive work a day.[36] He became interested in how the performance of his own staff interacted with pressures from outside the workplace and whether they would deliver more productivity if they had more time for themselves.

A month of planning preceded the trial, which was evaluated by local universities. Having more time away from work was found to improve workers' wellbeing and quality of life. They could do chores on their day off, freeing up 'quality time' to spend at the weekend with friends, family or by themselves and feeling 'less psychologically rushed'. It transpired that many employees saw reduced working hours as a gift from the company – 'a privilege not a right' – and felt 'a deep sense of goodwill and reciprocity', which made them 'willing to go the extra mile' for their employer and even work on their day off if necessary. A key result was that staff became much more engaged in their work and said they felt more empowered, as well as reporting higher levels of job satisfaction, collaboration and teamwork. The trial enabled teams to agree performance measures. Productivity slightly increased.[37]

Perpetual Guardian made the four-day week a permanent fixture from November 2018. Notably, this was on an opt-in, annualized basis, with teams first agreeing how to deliver their productivity goals and deciding whether these were best achieved over four days or five shorter days. The 'gift' could be withdrawn if productivity fell.

Emboldened by the trial results and extensive media coverage (which did wonders for his company's profile), Barnes has since established 4-Day Week Global, described as a 'not-for-profit community to provide a platform for like-minded people who are interested in supporting the idea of the four-day week as a part of the future of work'.[38] He has written a book on the subject and issued a 'White Paper' with guidance for companies wanting to try it for themselves. This acknowledges that work reduction isn't 'a magic bullet that will help you arrive at some sort of productivity and personal satisfaction nirvana', but if management, workers, unions and government get behind the idea, it 'could work across most industries and within most work groups'.[39]

Trial by Microsoft in Japan

Andrew Barnes's optimism seems to have been borne out by Microsoft in Japan, which tested a four-day week for its 2,300 workforce without loss of pay in August 2019. Takuya Hirano, chief executive of Microsoft Japan, said he wanted employees to 'work a short time, rest well and learn a lot', and to 'experience how they can achieve the same results with 20 per cent less working'. The trial reportedly resulted in more efficient meetings and more contented workers, while productivity rose by 40 per cent. Employees took 25 per cent less additional time off during the trial, office electricity consumption fell by 23 per cent and employees printed 59 per cent fewer pages of paper. The vast majority – 92 per cent – said they liked the shorter week.[40] However, at the time of writing, Microsoft had not yet decided to extend it beyond the trial period.

A coalition of interests: Four Day Week Ireland

Our final example is a national campaign, drawing together a wide range of interest groups, to promote reduced working time through campaigning and practical support. We picked it out – there are many other similar campaigns – because of its high national profile and its focus on potential benefits for the natural environment as well as for society and the economy.

Four Day Week Ireland (4DWI) describes itself as a 'campaign coalition of trade unions, businesses, environmentalists, women's rights and civil society organisations, academics, health practitioners and global advocates'.[41] Notably, it promotes reduced working time on social, economic and ecological grounds, offering support to Irish employers who embark on a four-day week because it is 'better for business, better for workers, better for women, and better for the environment'.

4DWI seeks 'a gradual, steady, managed transition to a shorter working week for all workers in the private and public sectors', and to 'change the false narrative that working long hours is good for productivity and a badge of honour'. It wants to make the four-day week standard practice, with no loss of pay, and envisages three routes to achieving that goal: business leadership, collective bargaining, and government leading by example and legislating where appropriate.

Learning from practical experience

Here we draw together key lessons that can help to shape an effective transition to a shorter working week. We look first at impacts on employees' daily lives and their quality of work. We then set out some implications for governments and trade unions leading the change. We consider questions of control, choice and inequality. And finally, we turn to factors that can shift the climate of opinion.

Impacts on workers' everyday experience

- In almost every case where hours are reduced, workers report improvements in their wellbeing and quality of life. They usually feel less stress and more job satisfaction, and take fewer days of sick leave.
- Working fewer hours without loss of pay makes the deal a whole lot more attractive to workers. For those on lower incomes, it can turn an otherwise unaffordable arrangement into an affordable one. Even payment of modest benefits to compensate for loss of pay can make a crucial difference. Reduced time without any compensation is more likely to appeal to better-off workers and to widen inequalities.

91

- Generally, workers like to have a fixed extra day – or specified extra hours – to do things that are not related to work, such as domestic chores, caring for family or otherwise pursuing their own interests. They appreciate being able to plan in advance, commute outside rush hours and pay less for transport.
- They are likely to feel less positive if they have trouble matching atypical work hours with established childcare and family routines. The same applies if they have to work much harder to get the job done and squeeze five days' work into four. This may depend on whether the employer is prepared to meet the cost of recruiting extra staff.

Impacts on quality of work and economic output
- In some kinds of work, the costs of cutting hours without loss of pay can be offset by workers improving the quality of their work (because they are under less stress) in ways that enable them to increase their hourly output. This may even exceed levels of output achieved before working time was reduced. In sectors such as manufacturing and financial services, it is a reasonable expectation. And there is a better chance of increasing productivity if employees are actively

– and collectively – engaged in working out how to get more done in less time.

- In other sectors, such as care, hourly output can be hard to measure, let alone to increase, through reducing work time. When carers' hours are cut, the quality of their work may improve, but the numbers for whom they can care are unlikely to increase and may actually diminish.

- Where reduced working time cannot improve productivity, additional staff will have to be recruited to avoid cutting the scope of the service or damaging the quality of work performed. Public sector employers may be prepared to do this – and the state may be willing to subsidize private sector employers who are taking on more staff – provided there is a public interest justification with returns to the public purse.

- In some circumstances, reduced working time can create more jobs for the unemployed so that fewer people claim social security benefits, or need treatment for the damage unemployment can do to their health. If unemployment rates are unacceptably high, the trade-off can be worth it, but if rates decline, incentives will be weaker. In any event, the costs of additional staff are immediate and certain, while the potential savings are less certain, longer term and often accrue to parts of the economy that did not make the original investment.

Initiatives led by governments and trade unions
- Direct intervention by government to limit hours of work can effect change across a population. But there is always a risk of political reversal.
- Whether innovations can be defended against retrenchment will depend on how far the effects have proved popular with workers, employers and voters in general, and how far the laws have become embedded in institutions and perceived as 'normal'.
- If employers and workers' organizations negotiate agreements about how national legislation is implemented locally, they are more likely to identify with the change and feel some ownership of it. This in turn can impede efforts by future governments that want to reverse the legislation.
- Well-organized industrial workers can be effective leaders of change. Campaigning for reduced working time can help to attract new members and reinvigorate union activity. Where there is a tradition of 'social partnership' between unions and employers, with some degree of trust between them, unions have been able to play a role as problem-solvers and innovators in hard

times, reducing hours of work with gains on both sides.

- A proliferation of collective agreements is bound to lead to a variety of arrangements for reduced working time, and may exacerbate inequalities by enabling some groups of workers to get a more favourable deal than others.

- A combination of national legislation and collective bargaining is thought likely to be more inclusive and spread the benefits more evenly, compared with reducing hours solely through negotiated settlements.[42]

Questions of control, choice and equality

- It clearly matters a great deal how much control people feel they have over their time. If they are engaged in planning the transition and have a say in how their hours are allocated, they are far more likely to support reduced working time. Changes that enable employers to decide unilaterally are less likely to be popular with workers.

- Agreements to reduce working time often include provisions for flexible working. Workers value flexibility if it means being able to determine their own time schedules so that they can better reconcile work and private life.[43] Yet rapidly changing technologies require them to be ever more adaptive and available at work. How far flexibility actually improves workers' lives will depend on who has the power to choose when they put in the hours.

- Where there are options for individuals to choose reduced working time, women and better-paid workers are more likely to do so – women because of domestic responsibilities that they cannot avoid, and better-paid workers because they can more easily afford it. An entirely voluntary system, especially where the option is to cut hours without pay protection, is likely to work with the grain of cultural norms and to leave inequalities undisturbed.

Changing the climate of opinion

- Where experience of reduced working time is piecemeal or temporary (as is often the case), it can still help to shift the climate of opinion by raising awareness and contributing to a body of knowledge about methods and impacts.
- Trials that are well evaluated can exert a powerful influence long after they have come to an end by providing evidence of their effects that is widely available to inform and encourage potential innovators
- Where trade unions are able to win early agree-

ments on reduced working time, they can start to shift expectations and embolden workers in other sectors to take action on their own behalf.

- Turning an official 'norm' into everyday normality is a long-term process 'that requires continuous intervention by actors at various levels'.[44] But while a new sense of 'normality' can be hard to build, once changes are under way it can be hard to reverse them.

5

A Road Map for Transition

We envisage a set of converging pathways towards a shorter working week. There are voluntary initiatives by pioneering employers and workers who show that an alternative to the status quo is achievable and point to some of the effects. At the same time, a range of partial and incremental measures, encouraged and supported through government regulations and workplace negotiations, create conditions that are favourable to change and spread experience of reduced working time across the population. A growing body of evidence from emerging practice informs further developments and feeds into campaigns for a shorter working week. A new consensus develops about what is 'normal' and desirable. Further regulations underpin these changes to establish new standards for paid working time as a universal entitlement.

Of course we can't be sure things will unfold as we imagine. Here we offer a set of parameters for transition, which should apply whatever routes are taken.

- *The transition is collective, for the benefit of all.* Although individual choices pave the way, the driving ambition is to change what is 'normal' for the whole working population. Anything less would risk widening existing inequalities.
- *The shift is gradual.* Our call for reduced working time belongs to a tradition of incremental change that goes back more than 150 years. A dramatic, overnight change imposed from the top is unlikely to produce good results. Workers, employers and their organizations need time and space to learn from experience and make necessary adjustments.
- *Pay must be sufficient.* No one should have to accept insufficient pay in return for reduced hours of work. Over time, people will exchange more time off for less additional pay, but this should only happen when they can still earn enough to afford to make the choice voluntarily.
- *The outcome is not uniform.* We don't expect or seek a one-size-fits-all model of reduced working time for all. People's jobs, families, living conditions and income levels are far too varied

for that to be achievable, let alone equitable or fair. Reduced working time must be flexible enough to meet a wide range of needs.

- *The speed and nature of change will vary.* Many office-based jobs are well placed to reduce hours straight away, while jobs requiring face-to-face interaction take longer to adjust. We must expect some sectors to lead the way, but we must make sure others are able to follow close behind

- *This is not a stand-alone strategy.* The transition to a shorter working week is part and parcel of a broader progressive agenda that addresses major structural issues, including wages, industrial strategy, welfare state reform and climate mitigation.

Within these parameters, we envisage a transition with overlapping components: preparing the ground, supporting innovation, strengthening and extending existing entitlements, changing the climate of opinion, embedding change and building momentum.

Preparing the ground

Independent action by groups and individuals is an important early route to a shorter working week

– already well under way – demonstrating what is possible and building knowledge and experience. Innovation can be a product of collective bargaining, individual claims or pioneering employers in the public and private sectors. It can also be stimulated by government regulations that encourage employers to adapt in creative ways.

Collective bargaining

Generations of trade unionists established new norms and expectations for the eight-hour day and two-day weekend around the turn of the twentieth century.[1] Then and since, working time reductions have typically begun in economic sectors with high union density.[2] Today, trade unions have significant opportunities to achieve reduced working time – to improve their members' wellbeing and avoid the threat of lay-offs as a result of automation.

Where possible, trade unions should seek to embed plans to reduce working time in sectoral agreements, for example those dealing with the effects of new technologies.[3] At workplace level, trade unions can encourage members to set up committees that campaign within organizations for shorter hours, raise expectations among colleagues, make the case to management and propose strategies for making the transition.

When it comes to annual pay reviews, one strategy for trade unions, discussed earlier (see pp. 49–50), is to negotiate a small amount of extra time off each year in return for a smaller pay increment to keep in line with (or above) the rate of inflation. If continued year on year, this would have a cumulative effect, with workers gradually reducing their working time without a cut in pay – although their pay would rise at a slower rate. It would need to include measures to reduce the pay gap between lower and higher earners and would preferably be a collective deal agreed across the workforce.

Individual claims

Successful claims by individuals to reduce their hours can, as numbers accumulate, help to shift norms and expectations about paid working time, and build good practice in the workplace. Employees should be able to choose the hours they work within agreed parameters, and employers should consent to them, unless they have a very strong reason not to do so. It is important that chosen hours are as flexible as possible, to suit the different needs of workers, including term-time shifts, sabbaticals and compressed hours, as well as a four-day week or its equivalent in hours distributed across a week, month or year.

Pioneering employers

Public sector employers at national and local levels can exert a powerful influence by taking the initiative to reduce hours without *pro rata* loss of pay. They can encourage other employers to take similar steps – especially where they can demonstrate benefits in terms of staff wellbeing, job satisfaction, reductions in sick leave and absenteeism, and improved quality of output. Public sector employers have substantial purchasing power and can drive up standards through the design of their procurement criteria, so that contracting organizations are obliged to follow their lead.

Supporting innovation

Governments can play a vital role by providing regulatory and financial support for innovations.

Supporting trade unions

The capacity of trade unions to bargain effectively for their members has been severely undermined in many countries since the late 1970s and must be restored. If they are now to innovate successfully in reducing working time, laws that have limited their power to organize and bargain should be reformed or repealed. Joining a union, participating in union activity and being able to confront an intransigent employer with a just cause should be seen as matters of right, not legal transgressions.

Employers with more than 50 workers, agency staff or employees across one or more sites should be legally required to recognize at least one union, while employees in smaller workplaces should be able to gain recognition by means that are reasonably swift and simple.[4] Workers should have a right to spend the equivalent of an hour per week on activities such as holding union meetings and attending negotiations and board meetings.[5] And those employed through digital platforms without employee status should be able to negotiate directly with and, if necessary, take legitimate industrial action against their *de facto* employer.[6]

Some of the best agreements for reduced working time have been achieved through established social partnerships between unions and employers, often including governments. This tradition has been strong in Germany (see p. 80–4) and some Nordic countries, but has all but disappeared from the UK and the US. Creating, reviving or strengthening social partnerships would certainly boost the power of collective bargaining to move towards a shorter working week.

A Road Map for Transition

Supporting individuals

Individuals who apply for reduced working time make an important contribution to the transition. But without regulatory and financial support, the gains are uncertain and distributed unequally. Governments should support individual claims by obliging employers to respond as constructively as possible. Here, we can learn from the Netherlands, where employers are obliged to accept a worker's proposal, unless there is a very good case for denying it, for which they bear the burden of proof. If they have not responded within one month of the worker's requested starting date, the hours proposed will automatically be accepted and implemented. In addition, regulations should specify that arrangements for reduced working time must suit the needs of the employee as far as possible, not just those of the employer.

Individual claims typically involve the employee taking a pay cut, which means it is most likely to be adopted by those already earning enough to feel they can afford it, or who are second earners in a dual-worker household. This widens inequalities between women and men, and between lower and higher income groups. Governments can soften the effect through subsidies to compensate for lost earnings, and/or by establishing schemes for saving wages in advance, or by banking time to be redeemed when time off is needed. The Netherlands, Germany and Belgium offer examples here.

Supporting employers

As rights for workers are established, employers should be supported and encouraged to comply with legislation, through fiscal and other incentives that work with the grain of change. This may involve adjustments to tax regimes for employers as well as government support for training and development. For public sector employers, rules governing pro-curement should enable them to require contractors to adopt shorter hours. And in countries such as the UK, where local authorities have little power to raise their own funds, grants from the national government should provide sufficient resources to enable public sector employers to pioneer change.

A formal accreditation system could encourage employers to adopt reduced working time. A range of accreditation schemes have been promoted as an aid to recruitment and a boost to reputation and organizational success, as well as a means of disseminating good employment practice. The UK's Living Wage Foundation, for example, offers accreditation to employers who can show that they pay a real living wage to all staff. It follows earlier schemes, such as Investors in People, launched by the UK government in 1990, which offers graded accreditation, updated at intervals, reflecting how well employers treat their staff.[7]

Strengthening and extending existing entitlements

A crucial element of the transition is to enhance existing entitlements and swell the ranks of workers who experience paid time off as a right rather than a privilege. The following developments would be under the auspices of an independent Working Time Commission (see below).

Care leave
Workers should have paid time off if they need to care for someone. In the Netherlands, for example, employees are legally entitled to take care leave to look after a sick relative, an extended family member or an acquaintance (including a housemate, neighbour or friend); as part of this entitlement, employers must pay at least 70 per cent of their usual salary, and at least the statutory minimum wage – for a maximum of two weeks for full-time workers.[8] An equivalent version of this scheme should be available to workers in other countries

too.

Increased paid statutory parental and foster leave
In all countries, paid parental leave schemes should
be extended so that they are sufficient and available
to all, including foster parents. It is worth noting
here that the US is the only country in the developed
world with zero statutory maternity leave. Parental
leave schemes should incorporate 18 weeks of 'use
it or lose it' caregiving leave reserved for fathers
(or those in a comparable role) during the first
two years of a child's life. These 'daddy-quotas' –
employed by countries such as Sweden, Norway
and the Canadian province of Quebec – have helped
reduce gendered inequalities inside and outside
the workplace.[9] Progress has not been swift, but
as fathers have gradually increased their uptake of
leave to undertake parental duties (and so develop
appropriate skills and responsibilities), it has helped
to shift the dial towards a more gender-equal divi-
sion of labour.[10]

Make public holidays additional to statutory
annual leave
Public holidays are additional to statutory annual
leave in most OECD countries, with the UK and
US as outliers. Nowhere should workers be forced

to take public holidays as part of their allocation of annual leave.

Tapered retirement

Older workers should have the right to reduce their hours incrementally over a number of years as they approach retirement. For instance, if they were to give up one hour per week every year from the age of 55, within two decades they would reduce their weekly total by 20 hours. Not everyone wants to go on working until 75, so individuals should be able to choose when to stop – within a designated range between, say, 60 and 80. Flexible retirement could be aligned with 'time-banking' schemes, whereby workers opt to take time out earlier in their lives in exchange for working longer.[11] Provided that pension rights are secured, tapered retirement schemes could help to make more work available for younger people, for instance through apprenticeships. By offering a gradual reduction, they can lower the risks of depression and isolation that too often result from the standard practice of 'cliff-edge retirement'. A useful example is offered (again) by the Netherlands, where trade unions have agreed a 'generation pact' with the healthcare provider Fokus, allowing working hours to be transferred from older to younger employees, while safeguarding pension rights.[12]

Changing the climate of opinion

Entrenched views about what is 'normal' are known to be a formidable barrier to a shorter working week. A key component of the transition is therefore to build a new consensus by making the case for reduced working time, showing why it is necessary, what benefits it brings and how it can be achieved.

This is a job for trade unions and campaigning organizations, as well as for public institutions and supportive employers. They can spread the word about progress made so far, about official support for decent hours of work, about evidence of the effects on wellbeing, quality of work and productivity, and about innovations and good practice in different countries.

For example, this could be a good time to popularize and celebrate the UDHR on the 'right to rest and leisure', and the achievements of the eight-hour movement and subsequent gains in hours reduction, such as parental leave and extra bank holidays. Public health authorities could use techniques developed through campaigns on smoking, diet and alcohol to raise awareness of the health risks of over-long work regimes. Governments could take a leaf out of Japan's book, where employers were encouraged by the ministry of economy, trade and industry to let their workers come in at lunchtime on once-a-month 'Shining Mondays' to achieve a better work–life balance.[13]

As practical experience accumulates, evidence of what works (and what doesn't work) can be disseminated by unions, employers, policymakers, public authorities, academics and media. One example of campaigning is 4-Day Week Global, launched by Perpetual Guardian (see pp. 86–9). Another, related, example is Four Day Week Ireland (4DWI), which brings together trade unions and a broad range of social, economic and environmental organizations (see pp. 89–90).

Embedding change and building momentum

To ensure that the transition to reduced working time is as inclusive and fair as possible, an institutional framework is required to monitor progress, set and enforce standards, and provide momentum for further change. We propose the following components.

111

A Road Map for Transition

Establish independent oversight

An independent body – a Working Time Commission – should be created that recommends annual increases in statutory paid leave, on a similar basis to the way in which minimum wages are recommended and set in many countries across Europe. This would conduct independent expert analysis of the labour market and receive a mandate from government to recommend regular increases in statutory leave that are as high as possible, without having a negative impact on employment and pay. The Commission would review and recommend all changes to paid time off. Its mandate would be to map out a consensual path towards increased statutory paid time off in return for slower future pay growth overall.

Mandate a living wage for a shorter working week

Governments should establish a legally enforceable minimum 'living wage' within the context of reduced working time. This would set an hourly rate that makes it possible to earn a sufficient income by working the equivalent of 30 hours a week.

Measure working time accurately

Employers should be compelled to establish systems that accurately measure and report on the working time of their employees. These figures should be made public to ensure full compliance with prevailing legislation. Job-seekers would be able to make a better-informed judgement about an organization's employment practices before accepting an offer, and employers may be encouraged to offer reduced working time in order to attract talent. This would accord with the ruling of the European Court of Justice in May 2019, which obliged companies to set up a system to record employees' daily hours of work as a necessary condition for enforcing legal limits on working time.[14]

Integrate reduced working time with other policy programmes

Reduced working time should be integrated into local and national policy programmes and development plans. There's a huge range of opportunities here, including national industrial strategies, climate mitigation schemes and local community development plans – all involving new and/or reorganized employment.

For example, community wealth-building schemes, such as the 'Preston model' in the UK[15] and the 'Cleveland model' in the US,[16] aim to reorganize local economies to maximize local circulation of wealth and income, and minimize extraction by externally based corporations. Public sector employers and other local 'anchor institutions' are encouraged to invest locally and use their purchasing power to improve working conditions and service quality for the benefit of local people. Agreements with local contractors should include stipulations for working time reduction and decent rates of pay.

The Green New Deal (see 23, 38) is both a plan and a growing global movement to achieve a 'just transition' to a sustainable economy.[17] Investment in new, low-carbon jobs is a central part of that transition. It should become standard practice, for social as well as environmental reasons, for new jobs to be created on the basis of a shorter working week with guarantees of a living wage.

In a similar vein, there are calls in some quarters for a new social partnership organization to target investment in new technologies so that gains are fairly shared across the workforce, with reduced hours and protected pay.[18] And proposals for universal basic services (UBS) involve a range of jobs in care, housing, transport and elsewhere, to ensure everyone has access to life's essentials according to need not ability to pay.[19] Here, too, the default model for employment should be a shorter working week and a living wage.

A Road Map for Transition

Set limits for working hours

A critical function of government is to ensure that reduced working time is fairly distributed and genuinely accessible to all. This means introducing statutory measures to establish universal standards and entitlements.

Governments should legislate to curb excessive hours by setting a maximum weekly limit. Where there is a Working Time Commission (or equivalent – see above) this should be part of its remit, aligning progressive reduction in working hours with levels of productivity in the economy. The European Union's Working Time Directive, which limits working time to 48 hours a week for all employees, including the self-employed with 'worker' status, could provide a useful starting point – with further reductions reflecting subsequent developments in the economy. Establishing an upper limit should help put an end to excessive and involuntary overtime and discourage workplace cultures that associate long working hours with success.

Upper limits on working time must include the right to disconnect from work-related tasks out-of-hours. The point here is to stop paid employment from encroaching on leisure time through electronic communications such as emails or messages. France was the first country to incorporate this 'right to disconnect' into law in 2017,[20] and has since been followed by Italy and the Philippines.[21]

An important corollary to maximum limits on working time is to ensure that every worker has a right to secure minimum hours. The UK's Living Wage Foundation offers a useful pointer with its Living Hours campaign, designed to combat zero-hours contracts and other forms of precarious labour. This calls on employers to provide workers with the right to at least four weeks' notice of shift times, guaranteed payment if shifts are cancelled, a contract reflecting accurate hours worked, and a guaranteed minimum of 16 hours a week (unless the worker requests otherwise).[22]

In Conclusion

As we were writing this book, we experienced the unprecedented disruption of social and economic norms brought on by the COVID-19 pandemic. In the course of a few months, our ideas about shorter and more flexible hours of paid work took on new meanings and significance. Suddenly, going out to work for five full days a week became the exception rather than the rule. It was more common to work from home or not to work at all – either with or without wages. While 'key workers', such as those in healthcare and food shops, continued to go to work, many others got used to spending more time with their families. Fathers taking their children out for exercise became a familiar sight. Some people enjoyed the new arrangements; others found them intolerable. In many countries, it became widely acknowledged that there would be no return to 'business as usual', but instead there would be a 'new normal' of some kind that couldn't yet be specified. An extraordinary economic downturn – like no other in at least two centuries – was under way. Some countries would fare better than others, but a profound global recession was generally thought to be unavoidable.

As governments struggled to end their lockdown regimes and avoid resurgence of the virus (which remained poorly understood), they began to consider extending home working and staggering hours of work outside the home, to avoid commuter rush hours and maintain physical distancing in the workplace. At the same time the number of workers who knew what it felt like to have more free time rose dramatically, as did the number of employers with experience of reorganizing staff time. Meanwhile, it became increasingly clear that people who were relatively poor and powerless before the crisis were bearing a hugely disproportionate share of its negative effects – through greater exposure to the virus itself, as well as through indirect effects such as loss of jobs and income, delayed healthcare for other illnesses and enforced living conditions that threatened mental and physical wellbeing.

The pandemic and its aftermath have made it all the more urgent to move towards a shorter working week in the ways we have suggested. There are several compelling reasons why this is so. First, it could ease the transition towards ways of working that minimize risks of spreading disease. Second, it could enable more people to have at least some paid work in a period of high unemployment that may continue for some time. Third, it builds on new experience – among workers and employers – of working differently, and spending more time outside the workplace. Last, but not least, if the principles and process of transition that we have outlined are followed, especially those wider measures relating to pay and control over how time is allocated, it is more likely that reduced working time will help to reduce social and economic inequalities.

Here, in a nutshell, are the key points of our argument:

1 Everyone should be able to earn a decent living while working a significantly shorter working week than the current full-time average. This might be four days or 30 hours a week, or the equivalent spread across a month, year or working lifetime. This continues a long tradition of winning better conditions for workers to improve their wellbeing.

2 A shorter working week reduces stress and

anxiety and safeguards mental health. It frees up time for unpaid work, such as care and household provisioning, which provides essential support for society, while also creating considerable value.

3 Redistributing paid and unpaid time helps to promote gender equalities and makes more time available for community-based activities and political engagement,

4 Reduced working time provides opportunities for cutting harmful GHG emissions and wasteful exploitation of natural resources through 'convenience' consumerism, and makes it easier for people to live more sustainably.

5 As labour markets adjust to automation and other changes in the wider economy, a shorter working week can help to distribute employment opportunities more evenly across the population. In some sectors, reduced working time enables workers to increase hourly output and boost productivity. In all sectors, it can improve the quality of people's work.

6 Reduced working time must be accompanied by measures to combat low pay. A real living wage should be established that is compatible with a significantly shorter working week. Measures to reduce hours across the working population

should, as far as possible, maintain existing levels of pay, even if they encourage slower increases in future pay growth in exchange for more paid time off.

7 Practical experience shows that workers almost invariably welcome reduced working time, but want control over how that time is allocated. Our aim is to ensure that everyone is able to choose their hours to suit their needs and circumstances.

8 It's time to change what is 'normal' and make part time the new full time. The transition must be incremental, achieved through a combination of government interventions, trade union negotiations and pioneering employers in the public and private sectors.

9 We propose a new independent Working Time Commission to review evidence and recommend improvements to paid leave for all, as well as sufficient pay and maximum hours of paid work.

10 Moving to a shorter working week won't work miracles on its own. It must be part of a broader policy agenda that aims to improve wellbeing for all and create a safe and just space for humanity within the limits of the natural environment.

Notes

Chapter 1   Introduction

1 J. Walker and R. Fontinha (2019), *Four Better or Four Worse?* Research White Paper. Reading: Henley Business School, p. 8. https://assets.henley.ac.uk/defaultUploads/Journalists-Regatta-2019-White-Paper-FINAL.pdf?

2 C. Ibbetson (2019), 'Business backs a four-day working week', Yougov. https://yougov.co.uk/topics/finance/articles-reports/2019/09/23/business-backs-four-day-working-week.

3 R. Skidelsky and E. Skidelsky (2013), *How Much Is Enough? The Love of Money, and the Case for the Good Life*. London: Penguin, pp. 29–30.

4 TUC (2019), *A Future that Works for Working People*. London: TUC. https://www.tuc.org.uk/sites/default/files/FutureofWorkReport1.pdf.

5 D. Sage (2019), 'Unemployment, wellbeing and the power of the work ethic: Implications for social policy', *Critical Social Policy* 39(2): 205–228.

6 Letters to the Editor (2019), 'Future of the NHS and Labour's four-day week', *The Times*. https://www.thetimes.co.uk/article/future-of-the-nhs-and-labour-s-four-day-week-hs0f6qknj.

7　See E. Aveling (1890), 'The eight-hour working day', *Time*, pp. 632–638. https://www.marxists.org/history/international/social-democracy/time/aveling-june.htm.

8　K. Marx (1894), *Capital, Volume 3*. London: Penguin, ch. 48.

9　The Green Institute (2016), *Can Less Work Be More Fair? A Discussion Paper on Universal Basic Income and Shorter Working Week*. https://www.greeninstitute.org.au/publications/less-work-more-fair/.

10　'C001 – Hours of Work (Industry) Convention, 1919'. https://www.ilo.org/dyn/normlex/en/f?p=NORMLEXPUB:12100:0::NO::P12100_ILO_CODE:C001.

11　B. K. Hunnicutt (1984), 'The end of shorter hours', *Labor History* 25(3): 373–404.

12　B. K. Hunnicutt (1996), *Kellogg's Six-Hour Day*. Philadelphia, PA: Temple University Press.

13　A. Martin (2019) 'Insecure work: Are we at the tipping point?'. https://neweconomics.org/2019/06/insecure-work-are-we-at-tipping-point.

14　E. H. Gary, quoted in (1926), 'Attitude of certain employers to 5-day week', *Monthly Labor Review* 23(6): 16–17.

15　T. Messer-Kruse (2011), *The Trial of the Haymarket Anarchists: Terror and Justice in the Gilded Age*. New York: Springer.

16　E. P. Thompson (1967), 'Time, work-discipline, and industrial capitalism', *Past & Present* 38: 56–97.

17　B. Adam (2013), 'Clock time: Tyrannies and alternatives', in A. Coote and J. Franklin, *Time on Our Side*. London: New Economics Foundation, pp. 35–36.

18　A. Coote and S. Lyall (2013), *Strivers v. Skivers: The Workless Are Worthless*. London: New Economics Foundation. https://libcom.org/files/Strivers_vs._skivers_full-publication.pdf.

19　E. Musk (2018), Tweet, 26 November. https://twitter.com/elonmusk/status/1067173497909141504.

20 J. Ma (2019), 'Jack Ma endorses China's controversial 12 hours a day, 6 days a week work culture', *CNN Business.* https://edition.cnn.com/2019/04/15/business/jack-ma-996-china/index.html.

21 OECD data (2018). https://data.oecd.org/lprdty/gdp-per-hour-worked.htm.

Chapter 2   Why We Need a Shorter Working Week

1 W. Stronge and A. Harper (eds) (2019), *The Shorter Working Week: A Radical and Pragmatic Proposal.* Hampshire: Autonomy. http://autonomy.work/wp-content/uploads/2019/01/Shorter-working-week-final.pdf.

2 Health and Safety Executive (2018), *Work-Related Stress, Anxiety and Depression Statistics in Great Britain, 2017.* http://www.hse.gov.uk/statistics/causdis/stress.pdf.

3 T. Yamauchi, T. Yoshikawa, M. Takamoto, T. Sasaki, S. Matsumoto, ... M. Takahashi (2017), 'Overwork-related disorders in Japan: Recent trends and development of a national policy to promote preventive measures', *Industrial Health* 55: 293–302.

4 J. Kodz, S. Davis, D. Lain, M. Strebler, J. Rick, ... N. Meager (2003), *Working Long Hours: A Review of the Evidence. Volume 1 – Main Report*, Employment Relations Research Series No. 16: Institute for Employment Studies.

5 ONS (2018), *Labour Market Economic Commentary: August 2018.* https://www.ons.gov.uk/employmentandlabourmarket/peopleinwork/employmentandemployeetypes/articles/labourmarketeconomiccommentary/august2018.

6 S. Devlin (2016), *Massive Surge in London's Gig Economy.* London: New Economics Foundation. https://neweconomics.org/2016/12/massive-surge-londons-gig-economy.

7 M. Lawrence, C. Roberts and L. King (2017), *Managing Automation: Employment, Inequality and Ethics in the Digital Age.* London: IPPR. http://www.ippr.org/publications/managing-automation.

8   M. Marmot (2010), *Fair Society Healthy Lives*. London: Institute of Health Equity. http://www.instituteofhealtheq uity.org/resources-reports/fair-society-healthy-lives-the-ma rmot-review/fair-society-healthy-lives-full-report-pdf.pdf.

9   R. G. Wilkinson and K. Pickett (2010), *The Spirit Level: Why Greater Equality Makes Societies Stronger*. New York: Bloomsbury Press.

10   A. Coote (2012), 'Growing the core economy: Gender, time and sustainable development', *Local Economy* 27(8): 788–795.

11   A. Coote and N. Goodwin (2010), *The Great Transition: Social Justice and the Core Economy*. London: New Economics Foundation. https://neweconomics.org/uplo ads/files/82c90c4bb4d6147dc3_1fm6bxppl.pdf.

12   Coote and Goodwin, *The Great Transition*.

13   J. M. da Silva (2019), 'Why you should care about unpaid care work', *OECD Development Matters*. https://oecd-development-matters.org/2019/03/18/why-you-should-ca re-about-unpaid-care-work/.

14   ONS (2016), *Women Shoulder the Responsibility of Unpaid Work*. https://www.ons.gov.uk/employmentan dlabourmarket/peopleinwork/earningsandworkinghou rs/articles/womenshouldertheresponsibilityofunpaidwo rk/2016-11-10.

15   ONS, *Women Shoulder the Responsibility of Unpaid Work*.

16   M. Quinn and P. Smith (2018), 'Gender, work, and health', *Annals of Work Exposures and Health* 62(4): 389–392.

17   ONS (2019), *Labour Market Economic Commentary: April 2019*. https://www.ons.gov.uk/employmentandlab ourmarket/peopleinwork/employmentandemployeetypes/ articles/labourmarketeconomiccommentary/april2019.

18   Joseph Rowntree Foundation (2016), *UK Poverty: Causes, Costs and Solutions*. https://www.jrf.org.uk/report/uk poverty causes-costs-and-solutions.

19   E. Karagiannaki and T. Burchardt (2020), *Intra Household*

Inequality and Adult Material Deprivation in Europe. London: LSE, CASE. https://sticerd.lse.ac.uk/dps/case/cp/casepaper218.pdf.

20 A. Coote and J. M. Himmelweit (2013), 'The problem that has no name: Work, care and time', *Soundings: A Journal of Politics and Culture* 54: 90–103.

21 Coote and Himmelweit, 'The problem that has no name'.

22 J. M. Himmelweit, A. Coote and J. Hough (2014), *The Value of Childcare: Quality, Cost and Time.* London: New Economics Foundation. https://neweconomics.org/uploads/files/d38d274699e1ad7438_jxm6i2v5l.pdf.

23 Himmelweit, Coote and Hough, *The Value of Childcare*, pp. 21–22.

24 D. Boyle, A. Coote, C. Sherwood and J. Slay (2010), *Right Here, Right Now: Taking Co-production into the Mainstream.* London: Nesta, p. 13.

25 R. M. Ryan, K. Warren Brown and J. Bernstein (2010), 'Weekends, work, and well-being: Psychological need satisfactions and day of the week effects on mood, vitality, and physical symptoms', *Journal of Social and Clinical Psychology* (29)1: 95–122.

26 J. Nässén, and J. Larsson (2015), 'Would shorter working time reduce greenhouse gas emissions? An analysis of time use and consumption in Swedish households', *Environment and Planning C: Government and Policy* 33: 726–745.

27 F.-X. Devetter and S. Rousseau (2011), 'Working hours and sustainable development', *Review of Social Economy* 69(3): 333–355.

28 Devetter and Rousseau, 'Working hours and sustainable development'.

29 Devetter and Rousseau, 'Working hours and sustainable development'.

30 T. Kasser (2002), *The High Price of Materialism.* Cambridge, MA: MIT Press.

31 Transcript (2006), 'President Bush's press conference', *New York Times.* https://archive.thinkprogress.org/with-

recession-looming-bush-tells-america-to-go-shopping-mo
re-502f23e813a9/

32 I. Gough (2017), 'Recomposing consumption: Defining
    necessities for sustainable and equitable well-being',
    Philosophical Transactions of the Royal Society A
    375(2095). http://dx.doi.org/10.1098/rsta.2016.0379.

33 A. Pettifor (2020) *The Case for a Green New Deal*.
    London: Verso.

34 J. Fitzgerald, J. Schor and A. Jorgenson (2018), 'Working
    hours and carbon dioxide emissions in the United States
    2007–2013', *Social Forces* 96(4): 1851–1874.

35 Fitzgerald, Schor and Jorgenson, 'Working hours and
    carbon dioxide emissions'.

36 K. Knight, E. Rosa and J. Schor (2013), 'Reducing growth
    to achieve environmental sustainability: The role of work
    hours', *Political Economy Research Institute Working
    Paper Series, No. 304*. Amherst, MA: University of
    Massachusetts.

37 Fitzgerald, Schor and Jorgenson, 'Working hours and
    carbon dioxide emissions'.

38 Fitzgerald, Schor and Jorgenson, 'Working hours and
    carbon dioxide emissions'.

39 J. Schor (2013), 'The triple dividend', in A. Coote and
    J. Franklin (eds), *Time on Our Side*. London: New
    Economics Foundation, p. 10.

40 A. Fremstad, M. Paul and A. Underwood (2019), 'Work
    hours and CO_2 emissions: Evidence from US Households',
    Review of Political Economy 31(1): 42–59.

Chapter 3   Some Challenges

1 Term used to describe birdwatchers who travel far and
   wide to record sightings of rare birds.

2 N. Milton (2009), 'The terrible allure of twitching',
   Guardian, 25 January. https://www.theguardian.com/com
   mentisfree/2009/jan/25/bird-rspb environment-twitching.

3 UK Government (2020), *National Minimum Wage*. https://www.gov.uk/national-minimum-wage-rates; ONS (2019), *Employee Earnings in the UK*. https://www.ons.gov.uk/employmentandlabourmarket/peopleinwork/earningsandworkinghours/bulletins/annualsurveyofhoursandearnings/2019.

4 A. Coote and A. Percy (2020), *The Case for Universal Basic Services*. Cambridge: Polity, p. 7.

5 G. Verbist, M. Förster and M. Vaalavuo (2012), 'The impact of publicly provided services on the distribution of resources: Review of new results and methods', *OECD Social, Employment and Migration Working Papers* 130: 25–26.

6 Schor, 'The triple dividend', p. 15.

7 R. Skidelsky (2019), *How to Achieve Shorter Working Hours*. London: Progressive Economy Forum, p. 17.

8 K. Schwab (2017), *The Fourth Industrial Revolution*. New York: Crown Press.

9 A. Hornberg (2019), 'How localisation can solve climate change', *BBC Future*. https://www.bbc.com/future/article/20190905-how-localisation-can-solve-climate-change.

10 C. Ibbetson (2019), 'Business backs a four-day working week', Yougov. https://yougov.co.uk/topics/finance/articles-reports/2019/09/23/business-backs-four-day-working-week.

11 T. Jackson (2017), *Prosperity without Growth*. Abingdon: Routledge, p. 147.

12 S. Kuznets, quoted in OECD (2007), 'Beyond GDP: Measuring progress, true wealth, and the well-being of nations', International Conference, November. https://www.oecd.org/site/worldforum06/38433373.pdf.

13 Jackson, *Prosperity without Growth*, p. 121.

14 D. G. Myers (2000), 'The funds, friends, and faith of happy people', *American Psychologist* 55(1): 56–67.

15 J. Michaelson and S. Mahony (2012), *Measuring Wellbeing: A Guide for Practitioners*. London: New

Economics Foundation. https://b.3cdn.net/nefoundati on/8d92cf44e70b3d16e6_rgm6bpd3i.pdf.

16 Happy Planet Index (nd), 'About the HPI', http://happy planetindex.org/about.

17 OECD (nd), *Measuring Wellbeing and Progress: Wellbeing Research*. https://www.oecd.org/statistics/measuring-well- being-and-progress.htm.

18 K. Raworth (2017), *Doughnut Economics: Seven Ways to Think like a 21st-Century Economist*. New York: Random House, pp. 44–45.

Chapter 4   Learning from Practical Experience

1 D. Meda (2013), 'The French experience', in A. Coote and J. Franklin (eds), *Time on Our Side*. London: New Economics Foundation, p. 143.

2 P. Askenazy (2013), 'Working time regulation in France from 1996 to 2010', *Cambridge Journal of Economics* 37(2): 323–347.

3 S. De Speigelaere (2017), 'France', in S. De Spiegelaere and A. Piasna, *The Why and How of Working Time Reduction*. Brussels: European Trade Union Institute, p. 69.

4 Askenazy, 'Working time regulation in France', pp. 332–333.

5 Askenazy, 'Working time regulation in France', p. 330.

6 S. Lehndorff (2014), 'It's a long way from norms to nor- mality', *Industrial and Labor Relations Review* 67(3): 838–863.

7 C. Erhel, C. Nicole-Drancourt and L. Lima (2010), 'From selective exclusion towards activation: A life course per- spective on the French social model', in D. Anxo, G. Bosch and J. Rubery (eds), *The Welfare State and Life Transitions: A European Perspective*. Cheltenham: Edward Elgar, pp. 208–230.

8 J. Fagnani and M. Letablier (2004), 'Work and family life balance: The impact of the 35-hour laws in France', *Work Employment and Society* 18(3): 551–572.

9 Lehndorff, 'It's a long way from norms to normality', p. 846.

10 Euronews (2017), *Swedish Old Folks Home Abandons Six-Hour Workday Experiment*. https://www.euronews.com/2017/01/04/swedish-old-folks-home-abandons-six-hour-workday-experiment.

11 M. Congregalli (2018), 'Swedish researchers examined whether a six-hour workday is the way forward: Here's what they found', *Equal Times*. https://www.equaltimes.org/swedish-researchers-examined?lang=en#.X1DT6dNKhmA.

12 Congregalli, 'Swedish researchers'.

13 H. Schiller, M. Lekander, K. Rajaleid, C. Hellgren, T. Åkerstedt, ... G. Kecklund (2017), 'The impact of reduced worktime on sleep and perceived stress: A group randomized intervention study using diary data', *Scandinavian Journal of Work, Environment & Health* 43(2): 109–16.

14 Working 4 Utah (2009), *Final Initiative Performance Report*. https://digitallibrary.utah.gov/awweb/awarchive?type=file&item=27365.

15 L. Wadsworth and R. Facer (2016), 'Work–family balance and alternative work schedules: Exploring the impact of 4-day workweeks on state employees', *Public Personnel Management* 45(4): 382–404.

16 Working 4 Utah, *Final Initiative Performance Report*.

17 M. Percoco (2018), 'The impact of working time on fuel consumption and CO2 emissions of public fleets: Evidence from a policy experiment', *Transport Policy* 71: 126–129.

18 Percoco, 'The impact of working time'.

19 D. Jamieson (2011), 'Jon Huntsman's four-day work-week experiment comes to end in Utah', *Huffpost US*. https://www.huffpost.com/entry/jon-huntsman-four-day-week_n_873877.

20 Jamieson, 'Jon Huntsman's four-day workweek experiment'.

21 M. Pullinger (2014), 'Working time reduction policy in a

sustainable economy: Criteria and options for its design',
Ecological Economics 103: 11–19.

22 Pullinger, 'Working time reduction policy in a sustainable
economy', p. 5.

23 M. Debacker, L. De Lathouwer and K. Bogaerts (2004),
'Time credit and leave schemes in the Belgian welfare state',
Centre for Social Policy, University of Antwerp'. http://
adapt.it/adapt-indice-a-z/wp-content/uploads/2014/04/de
backer_lathouwer_2012.pdf.

24 P. Reick (2019), 'Why did organized labor struggle
for shorter hours? A diachronic comparison of trade
union discourse in Germany', *Labor History* (60)3:
250–267.

25 P. Berg, E. Appelbaum, T. Bailey and A. Kalleberg (2004),
'Contesting time: International comparisons of employee
control of working time', *Industrial and Labor Relations
Review* (57)3: 344–345.

26 J. Visser (2013), 'Database on institutional characteristics of
trade unions, wage setting, state intervention and social pacts
in 34 countries between 1960 and 2012', ICTWSS Database,
Amsterdam Institute for Advanced Labour Studies.

27 S. De Speigelaere (2017), 'Volkswagen 28.8-hour week',
in S. De Spiegelaere and A. Piasna, *The Why and How
of Working Time Reduction*. Brussels: European Trade
Union Institute, pp. 73–74.

28 Berg, Appelbaum, Bailey and Kalleberg, 'Contesting time',
p. 345.

29 P. Oltermann (2018), '28-hour week gains momentum
in German unions' push for flexible rights', *Guardian*, 9
March. https://www.theguardian.com/world/2018/mar/09/
28-hour-week-gains-momentum-in-german-unions-push-
for-flexible-rights.

30 Stronge and Harper, *The Shorter Working Week*, p. 63.

31 Reick, 'Why did organized labor struggle for shorter
hours?', p. 261.

32 G. Chazan (2018), 'German union wins right to 28-hour

working week and 4.3% pay rise', *Financial Times*, 6 February.

33 CWU (2016), 'Drive for 35', https://www.cwu.org/news/cwu-drive-for-35/.

34 CWU (2018), 'Four pillars of security and pay national agreement', https://www.cwu.org/wp-content/uploads/2018/03/0555118-royal-mail-national-consultative-ballot-low-res.pdf.

35 J. Jasper (2019), 'Royal Mail wins high court injunction to stop postal strike', *Guardian*, 13 November. https://www.theguardian.com/business/2019/nov/13/royal-mail-wins-high-court-injunction-to-stop-postal-strike.

36 A. Barnes (2019), TEDxAukland, 'The four-day week', 28 January. https://www.youtube.com/watch?v=xjgqCgoxElw.

37 H. Delaney (2019), 'Perpetual Guardian's 4-day workweek trial: Qualitative research analysis', University of Auckland Business School. static1.squarespace.com/static/5a93121d3917ee828d5f282b/t/5b4e425c8a922dd864bd18d0/1531855454772/Final+Perpetual+Guardian+report_Dr+Helen+Delaney_July+2018.pdf.

38 4-day week (nd), 'What are we?', https://4dayweek.com/.

39 White Paper: The Four-Day Week (2019), 'Guidelines for an outcome-based trial: Raising productivity and engagement', https://static1.squarespace.com/static/5c3e9f3555b02cbca8b01aab/t/5c6639880d929730b229a363/1550203293110/Four-Day+Week+White+Paper+February+2019+final.pdf.

40 P. Kari (2019), 'Microsoft Japan tested a four-day work week and productivity jumped by 40%', *Guardian*, 4 November. https://www.theguardian.com/technology/2019/nov/04/microsoft-japan-four-day-work-week-productivity

41 4 day week (nd), 'What it is', http://fourdayweek.ie/.

42 Lehndorff, 'It's a long way from norms to normality', pp. 856–857.

43 Reick, 'Why did organized labor struggle for shorter hours?', p. 262.

44 Reick, 'Why did organized labor struggle for shorter hours?', p. 258.

Chapter 5   A Road Map for Transition

1 E. Chase (1993), 'The brief origins of May Day', *Industrial Workers of the World*. https://www.iww.org/history/library/misc/origins_of_mayday.

2 K. Tijdens (2003), 'Employees' and employers' preferences for working time reduction and working time differentiation: A study of the 36-hour working week in the Dutch banking sector', *Acta Sociologica* 46(1): 69–82.

3 Stronge and Harper, *The Shorter Working Week*.

4 New Economics Foundation (2019), 'New rules for the economy: Three missions to transform our failing economic system', https://neweconomics.org/uploads/files/newrules2020.pdf.

5 New Economics Foundation, 'New rules for the economy'.

6 New Economics Foundation, 'New rules for the economy'.

7 Investors in People (2019), 'We invest in people framework', http://www.investorsinpeople.com/wp-content/uploads/2019/10/We-invest-in-people-framework.pdf.

8 E. Pluijm (2018), 'Work and care act: Types of care leave', *Russell Advocaten*. https://www.russell.nl/publication/care-leave-netherlands.

9 A. Dunatchik and B. Özcan (2019), 'Reducing mommy penalties with daddy quotas', *Social Policy Working Paper 07-19*. London: LSE Department of Social Policy.

10 R. Rehel (2014), 'When dad stays home too: Paternity leave, gender, and parenting'. *Gender and Society* 28(1): 110–132.

11 S. O'Connor (2018), 'Retirees are not the only ones who need a break', *Financial Times*, 7 August.

12 ETUC (2018), 'A better life for young and old(er)', https://www.etuc.org/en/better-life-young-and-older.

13 J. Ryall (2018), 'Shining Monday: How Japan is trying to

make start of working week more palatable', *Telegraph*, 2 August. https://www.telegraph.co.uk/news/2018/08/02/shining-monday-japan-trying-make-start-working-week-palatable/; J. McCurry (2018), 'Japan urges overworked employees to take Monday mornings off', *Guardian*, 3 August. https://www.theguardian.com/world/2018/aug/03/japan-overworked-employees-monday-mornings-off.

14 A. Harper (2019), *Achieving a Shorter Working Week Across Europe: Issue 2*. London: New Economics Foundation.

15 CLES and Preston City Council (2019), 'How we built community wealth in Preston: Achievements and lessons', https://cles.org.uk/wp-content/uploads/2019/07/CLES_Preston-Document_WEB-AW.pdf.

16 T. Howard (2012), 'Owning your own job is a beautiful thing: Community wealth building in Cleveland, Ohio', Democracy Collaborative. https://democracycollaborative.org/learn/publication/owning-your-own-job-beautiful-thing-community-wealth-building-cleveland-ohio.

17 M. Fahnbulleh and D. Powell (2019), *A Green New Deal: Why a UK Green New Deal Is What Post-Brexit Britain Needs*. London: New Economics Foundation.

18 C. Roberts, H. Parkes, R. Statham and L. Rankin (2019), *The Future Is Ours: Women, Automation, and Equality in the Digital Age*. London: IPPR; Stronge and Harper, *The Shorter Working Week*.

19 Coote and Percy, *The Case for Universal Basic Services*.

20 N. Boring (2017), 'France: Right to disconnect takes effect', *Global Legal Monitor*. https://www.loc.gov/law/foreign-news/article/france-right-to-disconnect-takes-effect/.

21 Senate of the Republic (2017), 'Legislature 17[a] – Bill n.2233-B', http://www.senato.it/japp/bgt/showdoc/17/DDLMESS/0/1022243/index.html; Republic of the Philippines House of Representatives (2017), House Bill No.4721. http://www.congress.gov.ph/legisdocs/basic_17/HB04721.pdf.

22 Living Wage (nd), 'Living hours'. https://www.livingwage.

org.uk/news/living-hours-campaign-launched-tackle-wo
rk-insecurity#:~:text=The%20scheme%20will%20require
%20organisations,of%2016%20hours%20a%20week.

Index

Index

Index

Index

Index

Index

Index

Index

Index

Index

transition to shorter working
hours 15–16, 49–50,
98–116
climate of opinion 96–7,
110–11
embedding change and
building momentum
111–16
individual claims 102–3,
105–6
integrating with other
policy programmes
113–14
negotiated agreements
80–6
parameters for 99–100
preparing the ground
100–1
strengthening and
extending existing
entitlements 107–9
supporting innovation
103–7
see also government
interventions; trade
unions
transport workers in
Germany 84
travel, sustainable 46
twentieth century
1980s 7, 8–9
the 'normal' working week
5–7
working hours 5–6, 8,
10–11, 14

UBS (universal basic services)
114
UK (United Kingdom)
Communication Workers'

Union (CWU) 80,
84–6
French working hours 65
Green New Deal 23, 38,
114
Investors in People 107
Living Wage Foundation
106–7, 116
local authorities 106
low-paid work 9–10
minimum wage 48
Preston model 113–14
productivity and working
hours 13–14, 54
statutory annual leave 108
support for employers 106
three-day week (1974) 62
work-related stress,
depression and anxiety
18–19
underemployment 20, 21
unemployment 10, 23, 24,
57
automation 21
COVID-19 pandemic
119
in France 62, 63
and reduced working
hours 70
reduced working time and
job creation 93
United States
9/11 terror attacks 36
Cleveland model 113–14
and French working hours
65
and parental leave 108
statutory annual leave 108
Steel Corporation 10
studies of well-being 58–9

147

Index